The following pages provide consumers a simulation of actual documents on record or public court cases gathered from internet research. Readers must be allowed to construct their own opinion based on the information provided. The motive is to also introduce pertinent information that escapes the general public at large.

ISBN: Paperback 978-1-64873-305-5
ISNB: EBOOK 978-1-64873-160-0

AF889114

**Printed in the United States of America**

**Published by:**
**Writer's Publishing House**
**Prescott, Az 86301**

Cover and Interior Design by Creative Artistic Excellence Marketing

Project Management and Book Launch by Creative Artistic Excellence Marketing https://lizzymcnett.com

# HUDCO Scam Series

*Book One*

**Delhi Andrews Ganj Land Scam**

*By Alborz Azar*

alborzazar.net

# Table of Contents

# Introduction

The HUDCO Scam Series encompasses a detailed account of my findings during the research to expose the truth of Andrews Ganj's land misused by the Congress Government. The monies used were obtained from MS SHOES in 1994-1995 on various misrepresentations/fraud/ concealing facts of the properties developed by HUDCO at the behest of the Ministry of Urban Development. However, it is very important to show my appreciation to those who have cooperated in exposing the truth. In the end, the sufferer is the land costing today Rs.5000 Crores, which still lies idle without any use because of the scam/wrongdoings by HUDCO.

The Modi Government admitted to the Supreme Court in 2019 that the plot of land in a prime location belongs to the government, which was given for HUDCO to use. The company has failed to achieve its commitments, further admitting legal liability. Nor has HUDCO made good on the decretal amount to MS Shoes. In this situation, and HUDCO's inability to pay MS Shoes, the other properties belonging to HUDCO can be auctioned. But because of COVID-19, the refund amount owed to MS Shoes is hanging in the balance; therefore, the Andrews Ganj prime land is still unutilized.

# Chapter: One

*Andrews Ganj Land Scam by HUDCO*

The serial of Soniliv; the scam 1992. Harshad Mehta Story provoked me to investigate the reality of Pavan Sachdeva, and the fall of MS Shoes in 1995-1996[1].

One evening while bathing, I was applying oil to my body when suddenly my mind shifted, wondering what might happen if I slipped and fell. It made me realize the fall could break my backbone or worse. But how could this be turned into a total fall? I once read Shweta Dalal's book and interestingly, it had all the episodes of the 1992 scam. The whole incident created a burning desire to learn more about the meaning of a scam.

As I am not an Indian author, but from another land, and writing fiction books has always fascinated me. So, when I ran across this story, it intrigued my imagination. Since my success has yet to be achieved, because of my editor and publisher Lizzy who also turned out to be a professional saying the story is good, but the wording needs editing. I took her suggestion, and we went back to the drawing board, so to speak. The series of books currently being

---

[1] (MS Shoes)

worked on is the RAHA Series of nineteen books in which all the characters and incidents are imaginary being fiction books but the slowdown in editing and publishing, I am going to work on researching Pavan Sachdeva. In the downtime, I needed something to keep my mind busy. So, I scoured the internet to find more about MS Shoes' fall and the reasons thereof; more so the fall of Pavan Sachdeva.

The first information I had to uncover was if Pavan is still alive, as the media kills off all the people who have a fall in one way or another. My research uncovered he had been arrested on 6 April 1995 and released on 21 April 1995. The company, MS Shoes changed its name to Tomorrowland Technologies Exports Limited and then had the name changed to Tommorrowland Limited in recent years. As the research continued, it showed no website for a company named under Pavan Sachdeva[2], who had been termed as a scandal by the media at one time. I could eventually determine that since there was no apparent obituary registered online, he must be alive.

[2] (Indian Today, 2013)

So, after the incident, Pavan must have gone dark, lying low in some part of the world. But then I found out there were many judgments in favor of MS Shoes and Pavan Sachdeva appearing in courts as the CMD of the company. The information gave me the insight to find his phone number.

It took me several days to decide if I should contact him about his event or leave well enough alone. However, after a few days, I decided the most he could do was tell me to leave him alone. And if he was a good man, maybe having someone seeking the truth might be a breath of fresh air. So, I took a leap of faith and messaged him. I spent a few days carefully crafting a message. The last thing I wanted to do was scare him off, thinking I was some hack just trying to start more trouble.

The message was simple: telling him I was an author and wanted to write a book about his life. Would he be interested in sharing information about MS Shoes? I wanted to know more about what had happened. I admit his response upset me initially. He wanted to remain in the dark, unpolarized from mainstream media.

He said exactly, “I have had a hard time, and have yet to recover. By the way, there was no scandal as named by the media. You must also be aware; I am a lawyer and you dare not say such words to the public. I will take legal action against you.” Needless to say, the encounter left me even more intrigued than before.

When he completed his messaging, I sat down and prepared a questionnaire, and sent it to him. He never replied and promptly blocked my number. So as an inquisitive person determined to learn the truth, I got a prepaid phone and contacted him again. I kept my messages short and told him to write the truth, that it must come from the horse’s mouth. However, it took some time and several prepaid cell phones to persuade him to talk with me and me alone. Finally, after talking with him instead of messaging, I explained the incident was not a scam or a scandal and he was wronged. It came down to begging before he agreed to let me write the story. After some discussion, he told me we could Zoom and talk in two weeks. The interview was scheduled for December 15th, 2020, for thirty minutes.

I knew in the back of my mind that thirty minutes would never be enough time; however, at this point, I would take whatever he gave me. It was afoot in the door to get the actual story. So, the conversation left me with two weeks to research and impress him with my knowledge. The idea of actually being able to talk with Pavan was so exciting. I spent much of every night scouring Google to find information, pictures, etc. The schedule left me little time since I was still working to complete the RAHA Series with Lizzy. I had even come up with titles for the book, as I could not locate on google or news that he was a scamster or that he was involved in any scandal but ended with something direct and to the point: “MS Shoes Fall Series” with the book name of “Pavan Sachdeva Struggling”.

By the time the book had been titled, it was time for our zoom meeting. Pavan scheduled it for 5:00 p.m. Indian time. Since I was ten hours behind, it was not a big deal to accommodate him; most of the world was working from home at the time, anyway.

Our meeting started well, Pavan was soft-spoken and seemed very genuine. After setting the call to record, I started by asking if his scandal in 1995 was exposed in the way Harshad Mehta explained?

He started softly, "Do you know the meaning of Scam? In case you are unaware, a scam is a trick, a ruse, a swindle, a fraud, a racket, a story, a rumor, information, perpetrating a fraud, cheat, and trick or swindle a person or affirm, etc. To clarify further, a scam means to get money or property from another person under pretences by gaining the confidence of the victim, also includes swindle, defraud.

"From the above, a scam can be anything. It is a slip in any work or transaction within the system or the parameters. The slip takes place when the opposite party or enemy breaks in deliberately and intentionally to destroy someone. If the success goes through, then it is not a scam and if one can save from the slip, the scam is not there. But if the opposite party continues to hit, the result may be treated as a fall, failing to inform the public at large because they would not understand or know the reality behind it.

"The scam can be by a political party, a political leader, by a bureaucrat, by a wife, by a husband in the relationship, by a priest in the background of religion. A scam can be by a public sector company, by the brokers dealing in the securities, by the Government making rules and regulations, and many more than all these can result in a scam if there is a slip. But many of them are not termed as scams unless the media destroys, or the opposite party continues to destroy a person. The scam can be by a law company, by a company against another company, by an ex joint director of CBI, or by police in the garb of law."

Pavan Sachdeva then stated it may be termed as a scam by HUDCO, which is on the records. This scam involved the Urban Development Ministry of the Central Government in the year 1994 by floating tenders concealing various facts of the properties at Andrews Ganj, New Delhi to get the maximum money against the properties. These monies were used by the Government to build residential accommodation for Government officers being used to this day. The scam was by HUDCO permitting various interest-free extensions to Ansals Properties & Industries Limited but declining to MS Shoes. The scam/fraud was by HUDCO selling unauthorized properties without any sanctions or approvals completed by the MCD, DUAC, and Fire Department of the revised layouts, and without having the title of the property in their favor on perpetual lease.

"Unfortunately," he continued, "our legal system drags the cases as the opposite party desires. Isn't that required to be checked? The cause is because of the litigation policy not being strictly followed by the Ministries in the garb of honesty. The scam is by HUDCO holding monies illegally of my company and earning interest on it at @16 percent compounded monthly. The scam is by Superintendent of police Sh. Y. P. Singh falsely arrested me.

"The scam is the underwriters not paying the amounts towards the public issue on devolvement of the same. The scam is, after granting permissions, the regulatory body squeezes the corporate to reach a failure. The scam is by the then Minister who let the stock exchange be closed for three days. The scam is by the then Minister who took the wrong action on the letter submitted by a Solicitor Company. The scam is by the then Minister directing wrong at the behest of a Solicitor Company to save the regulatory bodies. The scam is by the then Superintendent of Police registering a false FIR without any basis."

I sat and listened to him explaining the situation in silence, it all took me by surprise. I had always thought many of the governments around the world were corrupt, but never to this extent.

Pavan continued, "The next part of this situation deals with a scandal; meaning disgraceful, shameful, or degrading acts or conduct, slander. Scandal consists in the allegation of anything which is unbecoming the dignity of the Court to hear, or is contrary to decency, good manner or with charges some person with a crime unnecessary to be shown in the cause to which may be added that any unnecessary allegation, bearing cruelly upon the moral character of an individual, is also scandalous.

"Who had committed such acts, not me but many against me who committed such disgraceful, shameful, and degrading acts to bring down MS Shoes and me, but the problem, there is no legal recourse to such acts committed in India but yes if it was the USA, it would have been a different situation."

Hereafter, there was no contact with Pavan Sachdeva as he did not want to disclose anything further. The whole thing came to a halt, as he was the one who could tell me about the scams in India he named. Since I'd spent much of my life writing and researching information for my other non-fiction books, I took his suggestions to carry on my quest of uncovering the truth.

So, I debuted a lawyer to search for court records. The task was arduous since we were on opposite ends of the world. My research on Google located many court case details that provided documents, as well as newspaper clippings, Wikipedia, etc., and finally contacting Mr. Y.P. Singh, the key man in destroying Pavan Sachdeva, and also some HUDCO officers who I committed not to expose their names. Mr. Y.P. Singh was a lawyer now, but was not from any department in HUDCO; however, some information about him was available on Wikipedia. The evidence uncovered showed it was done at the behest of many large corporations and big industrialists of India, as well as the underwriters who did not want to pay on the devolvement of public issue. The court cases have been ongoing over the last twenty-five years. Ansal was another name that came up. I found various brokers against whom decrees were under execution of the company MS Shoes, including Mumbai stock exchange views, and documents from the SEBI.

The whole incident started me thinking that none of these legal proceedings had anything to do with Pavan Sachdeva. Other than that, he was the one getting shafted.

My time spent uncovering the truth turned out to be highly advantageous. It gave me the foundation to write on a corporate scandal during 1995-1996, MS Shoes Fall, and Pavan Sachdeva Struggling. I found overwhelming evidence that Pavan Sachdeva had been scammed, not the other way around. In fact, the stories on Indian scams, although not called or named as a scam by the media, are highly prevalent. So, all my research inclined me to write several books on this subject alone. By the way, this story is based on records: the scam of Andrews Ganj Rs. 5000 crores of land being unutilized because of this scam by HUDCO. This is in line with the ministry heading HUDCO not refunding the legitimate amount received from MS SHOES and earning interests @ 14% to 18% with compounded interest monthly on retaining monies received during 1994-1995. I also found misrepresentations/ fraud/ concealing material facts that had been admitted by Shri Ram Jethmalani in the year June 1998 during the government of BJP. The legitimacy was also admitted by the Joint Secretary Land with the government in February 1998 observing that HUDCO may have not disclosed the facts of illegal unauthorized properties with the "fear that the auction may not realize the full value of the property if the risk factors are highlighted."

The Modi Government admitted to the Supreme Court in 2019 that the plot of land in a prime location belongs to the government which was given for HUDCO to develop. The company has failed to achieve its commitments, further admitting legal liability. Nor has HUDCO made good on the decretal amount to MS Shoes. In this situation, and HUDCO's inability to pay MS Shoes, the other properties belonging to HUDCO can be auctioned. But because of COVID-19, the refund of the amount to MS Shoes is hanging in the balance; therefore, the Andrews Ganj prime land is until unutilized.

As my initial investigation continued, the amount of information I obtained was seemingly endless. Until the day I happened on the story of Pavan, my writing career comprised sharing memoirs of people with the world. But as the stories waned, I found myself bored and yearning to stretch my writing skills, so to speak. The meeting with Pavan fueled my fire to uncover the truth. I have thought a lot about that day; he carried a sadness in his eyes that stuck in my mind. My heart went out to him and his situation. He obviously was an honest man, stuck in a bad position because of frauds committed by HUDCO. He had spent twenty-five years of his life trying to prove his innocence, then when the truth was finally told, the perpetrators ignored the court rulings.

The serial of Soniliv; the scam 1992 by Harshad Mehta story begins with a financial scam in the stock exchange resulting in defrauding several banks. The present story is of Alipur Land in South Delhi later known as Andrews Ganj Land, which has turned out to be a scam by the Government later by HUDCO defrauding MS Shoes, a company held by 51000 shareholders promoted by Pavan Sachdeva. I had spent nearly two months researching the internet and court documents gained by my assistant. However, I must first convey great thanks to Googol. It can help so many readers and the public with extensive research on any topic. I used the word Googol because it was founded by Larry Page and Sergey Brin. Misspelling of the word Googol showed the number 1, followed by 100 zeros, to signify unlimited quantities of information. Later, the domain name was registered as www.google.com on 15th September 1998. I must salute my heroes: Larry Page and Sergey Brin as well as Scott Hassan, the original lead programmer who wrote much of the code for the original search engine but left before Google was officially founded as a company on 4th September 1998.

# Chapter: Two

*1943 - 1948 Alipur Land (Now Andrews Ganj Land)*

On 14 August 1947, the new Dominion of Pakistan came into being, with Muhammad Ali Jinnah sworn in as its first Governor-General in Karachi. The following day, 15 August 1947, India, now the Dominion of India, became an independent country. Official ceremonies took place in New Delhi, Jawaharlal Nehru assuming the Office of the Prime Minister, and Viceroy Mountbatten staying on as the country's first Governor-General. 15th August 1947 was a period of religious turmoil in India and Pakistan which resulted in the deaths of hundreds of thousands including Mohandas Karamchand Gandhi who was assassinated by a Hindu fanatic in January 1948 during a prayer vigil in an area of Muslim-Hindu violence.

Thereafter, India has had a long history of scams, even before India became a republic. Under Jawaharlal Nehru, there have been many scams involving relatively smaller amounts of money. Such incidents were condemned under the Congress government, but not much action was taken.

The city of Shahjahanabad, also known as Delhi or Dilli, was enclosed within a high wall. To the north were Civil Lines and the Mall Road extending to the Kingsway camp where the 1911 Durbar was held to commemorate the coronation of King George V and Queen Mary[3] as Emperor and Empress of India. To the south, and detached from the city of Shahjahan, was New Delhi; to the west and just outside the city wall was Paharganj, Karol Bagh, and Sadar Bazar; and to the east was the Jamuna river, which was the old settlement of Shahdara. The rest were degraded forests, rocks jutting out of the ground, ancient villages interspersed with agricultural land, and the ruins of old cities: Tughlaqabad, Purana Quila, Bijay Mandal, and Siri.

For centuries Delhi had been the capital of the Mughal Empire from Babur to successors of Aurangzeb and previous Turkic Muslim rulers of North India. The core of the city is called 'Lutyens' Delhi'. By 1950, the government began allowing squatters to construct houses in certain portions of the

[3] (Delhi Durbar)

city. Delhi is divided into nine districts. The smallest district in population terms is central Delhi. Delhi was a very different city in 1947, and it is then that Delhi grew in every direction.

The scam of HUDCO Place-Andrews Ganj started in 1943 and onwards. It was the most prime land of Delhi, which is situated in the South Portion of Delhi adjoining South Extension, Jangpura, Khan Market, etc. The subject land was part of Village Aliganj, Tehsil, and District Delhi, all being Government-owned land.

In 1943-1948, the land comprising 200 acres at Aliganj, later named Pinjrapole and again Andrews Ganj at south Delhi, was given by the Government to Delhi Improvement Trust under the management of Durga Singh, son of Dharam Singh caste Gujjar, who was a resident of Kotla Mubarakpur which was near Village Aliganj. The land was leased for five years to cultivate an area from 16.6.1943 to 15.6.1948. Another portion of the land was leased to Leela Ram Gair Marusi. This part of the land was also in possession of the PWD department (Public Works

Department) which comprised all the drains and a tomb.

Sh. K.C. Neogi was appointed from 15.8.1947 until April 1950 as Rehabilitation Minister in the first cabinet ministry under Jawaharlal Nehru as Prime Minister of India. From the year 1947 until 1952, Sh. Rajendra Prasad remained as Agriculture Minister; thereafter, Sh. Rafi Ahmed Kidwai was Agriculture Minister until 1954 when Ajit Prasad Jain took the Charge as Agriculture Minister who also remained Minister of Rehabilitation from 15.4.1952 until 24.11.1954.

In 1953, a heroic boy was born in a family who had been struggling to settle in Delhi after coming from Pakistan following partition and independence. As this boy was born, the tensions in the family for money started reducing. His father was a very honest person in all his business dealings but went through difficulties for a few years until he finally settled in by 1960. The boy was named Pavan by his family.

It was not known, nor could be guessed, that a poor boy born in a family whose father had a bicycle, later a scooter, and then a brand-new ambassador car in 1970 when he was 17 years old would be a problem for Alipur Land. The land was marked and being cultivated by Pinjrapole, a society sheltering cows until it was later marked by Andrews Ganj. But most definitely, this boy had zilch as he did his schooling from Delhi Public School; however, he passed in First Division in 1970 when the Andrews Ganj land was until in possession of Pinjrapole Society. He joined Sri Ram College of Commerce and completed his Bachelor of commerce in the year 1973 and obtained his law degree in the year 1976 when until Andrews Ganj Land was in the possession of Pinjrapole Society. Does nobody know what was going to happen next?

Sh. Mehr Chand Khanna was appointed the minister for rehabilitation from 7.12.1954 to 1967 during Nehru's time as Prime Minister of India from 1947 to 1964, then later under the Prime Ministership of Lal Bahadur Shastri. All kinds of schemes were hastily put together to find accommodation, start schools, find jobs, and process claims of compensation. Agricultural lands were gained and hectic construction began initially thrown together by makeshift arrangements to then build more permanent structures. Those with property papers had an advantage; those that had no documents ran from pillar to post, begging for a roof over their heads.

Cramped accommodations came up at newly created residential areas thrown up virtually overnight in Lajpat Nagar, Amar Colony, Jangpura, and Bhogal. This was in proximity to the shrine of Hazrat Nizamuddin, South extension all called south Delhi next to adjoining Central Delhi like Connaught Place, Khan market, etc., including Pinjrapole land. The concerning story of the doings by the Government and later HUDCO was the struggle to gain a tremendous amount of money out of this land by obtaining its freehold.

Starting in the mid-1950s and its gradual eclipse beginning with the dawn of the 21st century is the next big story in the life of the perpetual city. Meanwhile, the process of amalgamation of cultures, lifestyles, food, music, and attire that has defined Delhi for a thousand years continues.

Minister Mehr Chand Khanna, who remained Minister of Rehabilitation as well as Housing from 1954 to 1967, handled many resettlement schemes by acquiring and allotting these lands to big companies who grew into thousands of Crores rich. These companies were cartel-like, land mafias, but managed legally and are presently holding enormous amounts of land with the bank in India

# Chapter: Three

*72 Acres Prime Land Given to Pinjrapole Society for Ten Years on Lease for Rs.25000/ Per annum*

The details are necessary to expose the happenings of this valuable land at Andrews Ganj in the so-called system of honesty concerning officers and ministers of Congress government handling this land, which is continuing to the present date. As what is done cannot be undone by the current Government honestly trying to do its best.

After the lease of Aliganj expired in 1948, the K.M. Munshi, the Minister of Food and Agriculture allotted this land through the agriculture Ministry for ten years beginning in 1950. It was again leased to the same people for the reasons best known to him, only in the name of Pinjrapole Society by the concerned officers and minister. The land was allotted through the Pinjrapole Society. The Secretary of the Society was Padam Chand Gupta. General Secretary Bhani Ram Gupta was controlling the ministry at the relevant time.

These people approached the Babus convincing them that it was a Charitable Society in the name of Pinjrapole, and the main cause was to provide asylum to aged, sick, infirm, and disowned cows and bullocks. They had various unofficial meetings and got the land for Rs 25000/- lease per year for ten years. The Agriculture Ministry obliged Pinjrapole Society in the garb of being a Charitable Society to maintain old and sick cows and buffaloes. Interestingly, the lease expired in 1960. But they continued to sublease the land on rents, although was to be utilized for cows continued to misuse it for several years beyond the lease period while paying no lease fee.

# Chapter Four:

*Role of Delhi Development Authority*

After more information surfaced from my investigation, I decided the whole affair was an elaborate scam needing to be exposed. Now, I was even more committed to seeing this quest to the end. Indeed, Pavan had been correct on all fronts with this situation.

In 1957, the Central Government formed the Delhi Development Authority for the development of Delhi, whose objectives were to promote and secure the development of Delhi. According to plan, the Authority shall have the power to gain, hold, manage, and dispose of land and other property, carry out building, engineering, mining, and other operations to execute works in connection with the supply of water and electricity, disposal of sewage, other services and amenities to do anything necessary or expedient for such development and purposes incidental thereto.

The Ministry of Housing and Rehabilitation was changed to the Ministry of Works & Housing in which a Land & Development Officer was to control the development of the entire country in respect of lands and its developments. This office was to maintain records of all Nazul Lands acquired in 1911 for the formation of the Capital in Delhi and the land comprising Rehabilitation Colonies. Allotment of land to various Govt./Semi Govt. Departments and various political, social, cultural, charitable, educational, and religious institutions under the direction of the Government of India.

As with the decision to form the Capital at Delhi, the Lieutenant Governor of Punjab in his notification ordered the Collector of Delhi District to acquire land for the New Capital of India. After the land was acquired, Imperial Delhi Estate was created vide Chief Commissioner, Delhi notification. An Executive Engineer of PWD then did the Land and Development, known as the Land and Development Officer in the Chief engineer's office, under control of the Secretary to the Chief Commissioner in the Public Works Department. The Land and Development Officer was formally charged with the land record work and administration on behalf of the Government of Raisina Estate. The work was transferred under the direct control of the Chief Commissioner, Delhi, in effect from 1 March 1928. Thus, in 1928, the office of the Land and Development Officer came into being as a separate Organization under the Administrative control of Commissioner, Delhi. Since independence, the activities of this office have gradually expanded. In 1958, the Chief Commissioner resumed Nazul lands under the management of the Notified Area Committee, Civil Section, Delhi, and put them under the administrative control of the Land and Development Officer. The Land and Development Officer was brought under the control of the then Ministry of Urban Development (presently Ministry of Housing and Urban Affairs) with effect from 1[s] October 1959. Since then, it had been functioning as a subordinate office of this Ministry until it was upgraded to an attached office of the Ministry of Urban Development (presently Ministry of Housing and Urban Affairs).

The Central PWD was formed as the agency of Central Government operating throughout the country for planning, construction, maintenance, and repairs of all works and buildings financed from Civil Works Budget; including the renting and purchasing of buildings and estates when work is not functioning at the Directorate of Estate. The director of estate and CPWD are under the control of the Ministry of Urban Development. The director's role in the estate is to allot the flats/houses to Government Officers and Members of Parliament.

MCD, Municipal Corporation of Delhi has a role in Urban planning, including town planning. The MCD oversees regulation of land use and construction of buildings and many other civic responsibilities including sanction of layout plans, building plans, fire safety approvals in the building, and approving the completion certificate of the buildings constructed after building plans are sanctioned.

In 1973 to advise the Government of India in the matter of preserving, developing, and maintaining the aesthetic quality of urban and environmental design within Delhi. Plus, providing advice and guidance to local bodies in respect to projects of building operations or engineering operations or any development proposal which affects the skyline or aesthetic quality of the surroundings, and any public amenity provided therein. In the 1970s, uncontrolled high-rise development was the predominant concern. But in the 1980s, new concerns arose from issues linked with Asian Games, and then in the 1990s, the building of Dwarka froze the New Delhi Bungalow area. This decade's main concerns are about four issues: threats to the remaining oases of open spaces, riverine and forest; the need to improve quality of life in historic precincts; the need to ensure that dilapidated areas are redeveloped elegantly, and to find ways in which traffic networks can work efficiently but with a humane quality. The DUAC and Town Planner could construct without the approval of layout plans and building plans no buildings under MCD.

HUDCO (Housing and Urban Development Corporation) is a Public sector Company formed on 25 April 1970, fully owned by the Central Government under the Ministry of Urban Development. The name of the ministry changed to the Ministry of Housing Urban Poverty Alleviation by the present Modi Government. The object of HUDCO is to provide long-term finance to the companies. Over the years, HUDCO emerged as the leading public financial institution with a major aim of financing.

The subject land was later called as Delhi Pinjrapole Society. They were issued a show-cause by Delhi Development Authority to pay damages of the lease fee not paid and to vacate the property. The Pinjrapole Society went to the High Court of Delhi and obtained the stay, but the High Court was directed to deposit Rs. 25000/- (US Dollar 3333/-) which Pinjrapole Society did not adhere to and the stay stood vacated.

The subject civil writ was filed for quashing the notice of auction dated 15.5.1973 by the Assistant Settlement Commissioner who issued an advertisement in Hindustan Times on 20.5.1973 for auctioning on 22.5.1973. On the letter of Sh. Nathu Singh in the year 1977, a report of Patwari was sought by inspecting the site. The Patwari Kharati Lal submitted the report which declared the site Pinjrapole Society, was transferred by DDA to the Land & Development Office; therefore, the Land & Development Officer should investigate.

The deposit of Rs. 25,000/- (US Dollar 3230/-) directed by the High Court vide order dated 20.8.1973 in Civil Writ No. 773 of 1973 by Justice H.L. Anand could not be done by Society. Sh. B. Datta reported on 24.7.1974 because, according to the Government Pleader, there is no stay order in favor of Pinjrapole Society. Accordingly, in the year 1978, under the Public Premises Act, the action for eviction was taken. The possession remained with the Society illegally, unauthorized for another five years, unless Nathu Singh continued to write various letters and reminders to Delhi Development Authority.

Congress Government continued under Smt. Indira Gandhi when elections were held in early 1966 (upon the death of Sh. Lal Bahadur Shastri). She defeated her rival, Morarji Desai, to become the leader and thus succeeded Shastri as Prime Minister of India. In the period from 1967 to 1977, the Ministers of the Housing /Ministry of Urban Development were Sh. K.K. Shah (1969–1971), Sh. Inder Kumar Gujral (18.2.1971–22.7.1972), Sh. D.P. Chattopadayaya (2.8.1972–5.2.1973), Sh. Bhola Paswan Shastri (5.2.1973–10.10.1974), Sh. Kotha Raguramaian (10-

101974–1975), Sh. H.K.L. Bhagat (1.12.1975–24.3.1977), Sh. Sikander Bhakt (26.3.1977), and Sh. Ram Kinkar (28.7.1979–14.1.1980). All the ministers were dominating the bureaucracy by putting all the work on their shoulders, and the officers also jointly made hay out of it.

Sh. Jagmohan first gained notoriety during his stint as vice-chairman of the Delhi Development Authority in the mid-1970s. During this time, he grew close to Sanjay Gandhi, who wielded increasing clout in the functioning of his mother Prime Minister Indira Gandhi's government. During the Emergency (1975–77), Sanjay Gandhi entrusted Jagmohan with the "beautification" of Delhi, a task that involved large-scale demolition of slums.

Delhi Development Authority under the Vice Chairmanship of Sh. Jag Mohan issued damages against the Pinjrapole Society through Padam Chand Secretary by stating the use of land as agriculture. The unauthorized occupation from 7.9.1974 was also mentioned, further admitting it had come into notice for the first time on 3.1.1978, and the Land &

Development Office had transferred the aforesaid to Delhi Development Authority through a notification dated 7.9.1974.

In February 1976, the land was also reported to be encroached upon by various Jhuggies /shops and stalls. Sh. Jag Mohan received the report. On the subject complaint of Himachal Kalyan Sabha (Registered) Delhi, the proceedings of recovery were taken against the society. Interestingly, the Ministry of Works & Housing vides statutory order No. 1810, dated 20.7.1974, gazetted the subject land under the Nazul Lands Act at the disposal of the Delhi Development Authority. It was then handed over to the possession of Sh. B.S. Sethi, Officer of Land & Development Office, reporting the unauthorized construction at site No. 51. Pinjrapole Society was detected on 27.10.1974 as the new encroachment on 27.10.1974, and not as old constructions. The point to be noted is that land and buildings constructed on Andrews Ganj were unauthorized and in illegal possession of the Society since 1960.

I am until trying to figure out what made these government offices permit the ongoing illegal possession and continue to allow unauthorized constructions.

In December 1975, Pavan Sachdeva started his business as a young entrepreneur. His elder sister married Raj Sood in 1970 and became a widow in 1975. The shoe industry started as a small-scale industry by taking a place on the rent. Later, a partnership developed with his sister, and the business changed to a private limited company. His dream from day one was to grow big and form a large public limited company. Pavan was just twenty-two years old when he took his steps to start his own business.

A policy of small-scale industries was floated by the Government of India when Shri H.K.L. Bhagat was Minister of Urban Development. This policy was floated by Delhi Small Industries Development Corporation, which was building industrial sheds in various parts of Delhi. One of which was the Rohtak Road Complex at Nangloi in the west part of Delhi. Since his elder had recently become a widow, her name was used as a special scheme for widows. A single 1200 square foot shed was allotted in March 1976 in the name of Mrs. Anil Sood's and a deposit of Rs.5000/= (US Dollars 5.58 million). Another adjacent shed in December 1976 in the name of the company was allotted as a business associate company enrolled with DSIDC.

Of course, Pavan at the time did not know of his destiny, nor the scam of Andrews Ganj going on by Pinjrapole Society. The result would leave him caught in the stream of land and fraud committed by HUDCO, making him a scapegoat. Essentially, HUDCO and the government became very wealthy from his hard-earned money. But Pavan at present was a small fry, and he never thought or imagined anything like this ever happening. Nevertheless, he had big dreams like any other entrepreneur, including building his own Five-Star Hotel like Oberoi Intercontinental opposite his school.

# Chapter: Five

*Role of Vice-Chairman, DDA, Shri Jagmohan*

As my research continued, the evidence was overwhelming. I had suddenly found myself consumed with getting to the bottom of this whole scam. I somehow felt indebted to Pavan for allowing me to continue my quest for the truth. In all my years on this earth, my heartfelt calm while pursuing the plan to write about the HUDCO Scam Series.

In the period from 18 July 1975, the Ministry of Works & Housing in consultation with DDA put the proposal for the hotels, boarding houses up. The entire exercise was being withheld at the behest of big business houses and construction hotels in Delhi, in which the prime lands at Delhi were being eyed. Finally, these regulations in 1977 were approved and published on 15 June 1977, but only for the maximum benefits of the big business houses.

Sh. Jag Mohan was a famous man who became Minister of Urban Development in 1999 and had held the post of Lieutenant Governor of Delhi after his stint as Vice Chairman of Delhi Development Authority in the year 1978. The representations were sent to Shri Jagmohan by Sh. Nathu Singh Kohli, who was the Vice-Chairman, Special Area Smiti, South Area, New Delhi Chief of the Zone representing the residents of the area where Pinjrapole Society was situated. He sought progress in the eviction of the subject land. The Delhi Development Authority reported to him that the proceedings under the relevant section for eviction were going on and necessary action had been taken.

The Settlement Officer Sh. Jai Krishan Seekri reported through a letter on 17 July 1979 to the Ministry of Works & Housing that notice under section 7 (3) & 4 (1) are being served on the Pinjrapole Society by the Court of the Estate Officer/ Delhi Development Authority for eviction and damages.

The Settlement Commissioner reported that nine people are cultivating the land under reference. The people are sub-agents of Pinjrapole Society who started the court case is pending in the High Court against the Land & Development Office. It was further stated that, in the absence of the full particulars of the case, it is not possible to take any action against these cultivators.

The paperwork states, “Please provide full particulars regarding court cases and stay order, etc., urgently.”

The point to be noted here is that the civil writ was also against the Settlement Commissioner, who was also one of the respondents. He should have been aware of the subject of litigation.

Interestingly, it is a matter of record that the Court's information was sought from the Land & Development Officer by the Settlement Officer Sh. Jai Krishan Seekri with the subject transfer of site No. 51, regarding Pinjrapole society, Andrews Ganj, New Delhi to Delhi Development Authority in the year 1980. The site was called Site No. 51, Pinjrapole Society, Andrews Ganj, New Delhi. The Pinjrapole Society represented to the Land & Development Officer that presently has only 70 acres, which were transferred to Delhi Development Authority by the Government of India in 1974 for care and maintenance. The Society had already represented the office in order to provide alternative land in their letter dated October 1979.

The records of the lands controlled by the Land & Development Office were in shabby conditions and most unsystematically. On 29.1.1980, the Land & Development Office of the Ministry of Works & Housing informed the Delhi Development Authority that there is no record available on this site. But the Ministry of Agriculture executed a temporary lease on 5.5.1950 for ten years, yet the lease deed is not available. The original size of the plot was 202.21 acres. But at present, 75 acres are under the occupation of the Delhi Pinjrapole Society. The lease has been canceled by the Ministry of Agriculture on 3.5.1965.

Delhi Development Authority was inquisitive to get the land from Pinjrapole Society on 2.5.1980. However, a month later, the exact information on the court case by Sh. R.S. Sibal from the Ministry of Works & Housing, Land & Development Officer sought information from the Government Pleader informed on 3.7.1980. Interestingly, there is already a letter from the Government Pleader by Sh. B. Datta issued on 24.7.1974. Thus, the concerned officers at the relevant time, for reasons best known to them, continued to let the illegal possession remain with Pinjrapole Society.

The Delhi Development Authority officer Sh. H.S. Tanwar again sought information on 21.1.1981, stating the encroachment is residential and Delhi Development Authority had taken possession of said land on 19.7.1974. The encroachment is fresh and states no earlier action has been taken as the encroachment came into the notice on 20.1.1981.

Interestingly, Sh. Jag Mohan and the department had admitted in the year 1978 that the eviction action was taken against the society. It shows how the officers operated under the congress government.

Delhi Development Authority Settlement unit continued to issue various reports from 6.5.1981 until 22.10.1982, stating that encroachment is commercial/residential at Site No. 51. The Andrews Ganj directed the removal of encroachments under the letters issued by Sh. H.S. Tanwar, displaying honesty to his work or that he was not kept happy by the Society. But the same was not done on the plea. There was a court case that remained on flimsy ground and was excused. Otherwise, the stay had already been vacated as reported by Government pleader Mr.B.S. Dutta.

A letter was written on 16.10.1982 by Sh. Upendera Lal, Ministry of External Affairs to Delhi Development Authority to vice Chairman Sh. S.C. Khanna and Sh. Jag Mohan had become Lieutenant Governor of the Union of Territory of Delhi. The letter was requesting the encroachment at Andrews Ganj be removed since Asiad 1982 is approaching in November/December 1982. The encroachment will give a bad impression to the foreigners who will be staying at Asiad Village in the vicinity of the Andrews Ganj. This was followed by a letter dated 2.11.1982, but any of the authorities took no action even after Asiad 1982 games were over.

On 3.2.1983, C.S. P. Shastri wrote a letter from the Ministry of Works and housing from the Land & Development office to Delhi Development Authority to stop the encroachment on 74 acres of land at Andrews Ganj, followed by another reminder on 3.7.1984 by Sh. I. Chandhuri, but no action was taken. The Land & Development Officer informed the Delhi Development Authority that there is a court case of Pinjrapole Society which was fixed for 5.3.1984. The Land & Development Officer did not report the latest position sought by DDA on 8.8.1984. Furthermore, it was reported by the Assistant Settlement Office on 20.9.1984 and revealed that the Land & Development Officer on the matter, and the demolition squad were provided to the Land & Development Officer immediately upon request.

It was reported that the High Court passed the judgment on 31.7.1984, but the Delhi Pinjrapole Society filed an application that they intend to file an SLP. The SLP of the society stood dismissed by Supreme Court directing Pinjrapole society to vacate the Andrews Ganj land by 30 May 1985. In pursuance, the Delhi Development Authority settlement unit confirmed on 13.6.1985 that the entire unauthorized encroachment at this site was removed with the help of the Land & Development Office.

Junior Engineer of CPWD (Central Public Works Department) has informed the site to be handed over to CPWD by the Land & Development Office.

It became obvious that 72 acres of the most precious land in the heart of South Delhi remained an unauthorized occupation by the Pinjrapole society for the next 25 years. While pending litigation, the lease period expired and the Pinjrapole society violated the stay of the eviction. But it is uncertain who assisted in this land remaining idle until 1985. The only certainty: Congress Government was in control.

# Chapter: Six

*1960 until 1985 Prime Land Continued to be Illegally Occupied*

In this period from 1975 to 1983, Pavan Sachdeva saw many pitfalls in his business; running a company based on the shoe industry is completely labor-oriented. However, by now he entered exports that had their own set of struggles. Pavan then got married in 1979 to a noble but dominating girl, which he always appreciated. When he got married, he was already facing money problems. His export shipments were stuck due to the cancellation of a big order. Nonetheless, life goes on and they had their first girl child in 1980 and second girl child in 1981.

In 1983, Pavan Sachdeva got huge export orders from a big importer in Holland which was routed through State Trading Corporation as shoes were a canalized item. This business grew very big. He kept buying factories and developing them for larger productions. But until then, he was not aware of his destiny and kept growing. The Andrews Ganj Land scam continued, and they were not evicted from Pinjrapole society, which was holding the land illegally.

We must fast forward twenty-five years, as the Pinjrapole society continued to have this land in their possession illegally and unauthorized. It seems they are involved with some officers who stole the lease files from the agriculture ministry and Ministry of Works and Housing to keep the precious land for their illegal use, despite a stay reported to be vacated in 1974. The connections with the officers of Pinjrapole society, Government officers, the Land and Development Office, and DDA officers have allowed the precious land to be occupied without sanction by any authority. Anyway, none to be blamed, except the Indian System under the congress government.

All this happened in the period of Sh. Jag Mohan, the Vice Chairman of the Delhi Development Authority, was later appointed as Lieutenant Governor of Delhi, as well as Minister of Urban Development who was an honest officer/minister. However, he was surely not judicious in using his authority, as human beings do make some mistakes when they are in power.

From the records in hand, it has revealed that the Supreme Court of India freed the Andrews Ganj land so that the Government of India could use it for

General Pool Housing for the Officers of the Government, as stated by a filed affidavit.

After the eviction of the Andrews Ganj land from Pinjrapole Society, CPWD under the Ministry of Housing & Works proposed to construct Government flats on the subject land. Mr. B.B. Chakravarti, Senior Architect – I, CPWD, Nirman Bhawan to Delhi Urban Art Commission (DUAC) sent the Proposal on 2.3.1985 for construction of General Pool Housing at Pinjrapole. The General Pool Housing is meant for Government flats and allotment Officers to be considered by the Ministry of Housing and Works.

Construction was supposed to be started immediately; however, the available 29.74 hectares had no existing structure nor many trees worth mentioning. In 1985, according to the zoning regulation, a plan was submitted for a pocket area of 2.82 hectares to be earmarked and kept reserved for a Community Center for Zone F-3. It was further confirmed in the proposal to be considered at a conceptual stage. Interestingly, this conceptual stage approval sought in 1985 remained conceptual until the year 1998.

The DDA comments were sought per the Master Plan on the proposal for the construction of General Pool Housing at Pinjrapole (Land between Andrews Ganj and Sadiq Nagar), New Delhi is, however, at the conceptual stage. Interestingly, the proposal continued to stay as per the proposal and only shuttled between one department to the other for about 15 months after the eviction of the most prime land of South Delhi comprising 72 acres those acres were vacated by the Pinjrapole Society on 30 May 1985 as directed by the Supreme Court.

Before the date of vacation and the proposal submitted by CPWD, a clarification was sought on 22/26.3.1985 by the DUAC Sh. J.J.S. Majithia, Assistant Secretary (Technical) whether the proposal was to be considered at the conceptual stage, or else the same is being forwarded to the local body.

Sh. B.B. Chakravarti of CPWD replied, "On 2nd April 1985 to The Secretary, DUAC that as desired the block layout model prepared in a scale of 1:1000 along with three copies of its photographs is submitted herewith necessary further action at your end."

DUAC informed CPWD on 10.4.1985 that, "On initial scrutiny, it has been found there appears to be some discrepancy between the layout plan and the zonal plan indicated in the key plan. It will be appreciated if the matter could be discussed with the Secretary of Delhi Urban Art Commission to clarify the position preferably on 15th April 1985 after 2.30 p.m. or any other time with a prior appointment."

CPWD through Sh. B.B. Chakravarti clarified on 3.5.1985 to Sh. G.D. Mathur, the Secretary, DUAC that, "the doubt raised by you regarding the existence of discrepancies between the layout plan submitted and the zonal plan is wrong. On page 64 of the Delhi Master Plan, it clearly states that after the master plan is sanctioned, all new developments shall take place according to zonal development plans, which shall show the features in broad outlines. It should be noted that nowhere is it written the pocket of land to be developed should be a 'blow-up' of the zonal development plan. However, Zone F-3, where the concerned pocket of land lies, needs to be provided with the following community facilities as per Delhi Master Plan.

- Community Center–7 acres as per Delhi Master Plan.
- Local Shopping0.9 acres Standards (Page 07 Table 4)
- Two Primary Schools2 acres each.
- Parks/playgrounds for total open space15 acres (out of 15,000 population these 10 acres is for 'park').

The proposed layout plan incorporates the following community facilities:

- Community Center–7 acres of land located as per Zonal Development Plan.
- Local Shopping–0.7 acres
- Schools4 acres for two schools.
- ParksTotal area: 15.57 acres including tot-lots.

From the above correspondence, it reveals that there was the Master Plan under sanction at the relevant time and any new developments had to be exactly as per Zonal Development Plans under Zone F-3 as the Andrews Ganj land fell under F-3 Zone giving the Community facilities. F-3 Zone Plan.

Table 3: Shopping and other Facilities and the various Tiers of Planning Areas for Zone F-3

| | | | | |
|---|---|---|---|---|
| Population 1,50,000-2,500,000 | Population 40,000-50,000 | Population 12,000–15,000 | Population 3,500–5,000 | Population 0–1,000 |
| DISTRICT CENTRES | COMMUNITY CENTRE | RESIDENTIAL PLANNING AREA | RESIDENTIAL UNIT | HOUSING CLUSTER |
| Shopping 200 to 350 shops, facilities, and service industries and Government officers | No. of shops 80 to 100, library, Religious buildings.<br><br>Cinemas<br><br>Petrol Pump (Service Garage)<br><br>Shopping and Service Industries | Local Shopping 15 to 20 retails shops plus service shops, professional officers<br><br>Community Hall, | Convenience shopping<br><br>No. of shops 4 to 6 Primary School<br><br>Playground | Toilets<br><br>Nursery School |

| | | | | |
|---|---|---|---|---|
| | professional officers, health center, post office and Telegraph, Office, Telephone Exchange, Police Station, Fire Station, and Electric Sub-Station | High School, Parks | | |

Table 4: Distribution of retail shopping areas in Zonal Development Plans

| Site Residential density | Community Centre Including shopping, services industries, and garages, community facilities. | | Residential Planning area center of local shopping (including community hall) | | Convenience shopping in residential units (only shopping) | |
|---|---|---|---|---|---|---|
| Population per acre | AAcres | NNo. of Shops | AAcres | NNo. of Shops | AAcres | NNo. of Shops |

| | | | | | | |
|---|---|---|---|---|---|---|
| 21 | 115.0 0 | 580 to 100 | 11.75 | 115 to 20 | 00.50 | 4 4 to 6 |
| 50 | 113.0 | DDo | 11.50 | DDo | 00.50 | DDo |
| 60 | 112.0 | DDo | 11.30 | DDo | 00.50 | DDo |
| 75 | 110.0 | DDo | 11.20 | DDo | 00.40 | DDo |
| 100 | 8.0 | DDo | 11.10 | DDo | 00.30 | DDo |
| 125 | 7.0 | DDo | 00.90 | DDo | 00.30 | DDo |
| 150 | 7.0 | DDo | 00.90 | DDo | 00.30 | DDo |
| 200 | 6.0 | DDo | 00.80 | DDo | 00.20 | DDo |

# Chapter: Seven

*Supreme Court Directed Pinjrapole Society to Vacate the Land Granting Freedom to the Land*

In 1986, Pavan Sachdeva started a proprietorship firm in the name of his mother-in-law called Urmil Suri. He then changed the name by floating a public limited company with promoters' names of his in-laws. I, unfortunately, could not find a reason for this business venture. However, reading India Today of 6 April, it may conclude Pavan Sachdeva allegedly committed evasion on customs regulations in his imports. His name was in abeyance, meaning he could not be the director until the pending case was decided. So, essentially, he became Chief Executive of the company to overcome the difficulty.

The clarification Sh. C.D. Mathur, Secretary, DUAC sought to vide a letter on 20.5.1985 to the Director, Delhi Development Authority.

It stated, "The CPWD has submitted a proposal on the above subject at the conceptual stage. The information seems to not be following zoning plan recommendations. A copy of the letter dated 3.5.1985 is enclosed for information. As the proposal is at the conceptual stage, I would request to kindly intimate the comments of the D.D.A. at the earliest so this project could be considered."

Sh. V.N. Sharma, Joint Director, DDA vide Letter dated 18.7.1985 to Sh. B.B. Chakravarti, Senior Architect-I, CPWD:

"Secretary, Delhi Urban Art Commission, New Delhi vide letter dated F23 (14)/85-DUAC dated the 20 May 1985 has asked the comments of DDA on the proposal submitted to them by Works Department for the construction of General Pool Housing at Pinjara Pole (land between Andrews Ganj and Sadiq Nagar), New Delhi conceptual stage."

Sh. R.K. Goel, Urban Designer, DUAC vide letter dated 23.7.1985 to The Senior Architect-I, CPWD:

"Kindly refer to the DDA's letter No. F.1 (20)/85-ZP dated 18 July 1985 regarding the above. To expedite the proposal, kindly send two copies of the layout plan submitted to the DUAC immediately to the DDA to offer their comments on the above matter."

Sh. R.K. Kakar, Architect, CPWD vide letter dated 26.7.1985 to Sh. V.N. Sharma, Joint Director, DDA:

“Two copies of the layout plan for General Pool Housing are sent herewith as desired.”

Sh. R.K. Goel, Urban Designer, DUAC vide letter dated 8.8.1985 to the Sh. S.C. Gupta, Director, Delhi Development Authority:

“Kindly refer to this commission’s letter of even number dated July 23, 1985, addressed to the Senior Architect-I, CPWD and copy endorsed to Shr. V.N. Sharma, Jr. Director (Bldg.), DDA. The layout of the above was forwarded by the CPWD vide, their letter No. SA (H&TP)/I/188/84 dated 26.7.1985. The above proposal is pending with the Commission and I would appreciate it if DDA’s observations are sent immediately and by 15 August 1985 at the latest.”

Sh. M.B. Sexana, Senior Architect, CPWD vide letter dated 2.9.1985 to Sh. V.N. Sharma, Joint Director, DDA:

“The matter regarding this scheme is under active consideration in the Ministry of Works & Housing, and we hope to hear from them shortly. As soon as the clarification is received from the Ministry, we will fix up a meeting with your director (Development Control & Building) for clarification and discussion."

Joint Director, DDA vide Letter dated 3 /4.10.1985 to Sh. R.K. Goel, Urban Designer, DUAC:

"A request was made to the Sr. Architect, CPWD to discuss the project of Pinjara Pole Housing with Sh. S.C. Gupta, Dir. (DC&B), DDA. Sh. M.B. Saxena, Sh. Sr. Architect, CPWD in his letter No. SA (H&TP) I/188/83 dated September 1985 has informed that the matter regarding this scheme is under consideration with the Ministry of Works & Housing— and the meeting will be fixed up to discuss this project after getting clarifications from the Ministry."

Sh. R.K. Goel, Urban Designer, and DUAC vide letter dated 17/20.1.1986 to the Sh. S.C. Gupta, Director, and Delhi Development Authority:

"You are requested to kindly intimate the latest position and expedite your comments."

It seems a large-scale acquisition of land around Delhi was initiated by the Central Government in 1959 under the Congress Government for planned development of Delhi. To achieve this object, the Delhi Development Act (DDA) was passed, and the Delhi Development Authority was created. On 2.5.1961, the Minister Mehr Chand Khanna of Housing took a policy decision that all the acquired lands should be entrusted to the D.D.A. along with the responsibility of allotment in residential and commercial plots, including all Nazul Land and Andrews Ganj.

The term "Nazul land has a definite connotation. It inter alia means, "Land or buildings in or near towns or villages which have escheated to the Government; property escheated or lapsed to the State; commonly applied to any land or house property belonging to Government either as an escheat or as having belonged to a former Government."

The revenue document even shows Nazul land situated within the prescribed limits of the Municipal Corporation, and the Nagar Palika is stated as under "Nazul" and "Government land". It is that land, the property of the Government, that is not forming the records in the account of any village.

# Chapter: Eight

*Sh. Mehr Chand Khanna the Minister of Works and Housing Role*

It was decided by Sh. Mehr Chand Khanna, the Minister of Works and Housing said that the Nazul lands were being occupied by the Development Department of the Central Government. The property should not be allotted for residential or commercial purposes to individuals or cooperative societies.

In 1972, Minister Inder Kumar Gujral decided at the Ministerial level to impose a ban on allotment of any land in South Delhi. There was also a ban on the allotment to cooperative societies in South Delhi imposed in 1981 by the then Minister Sh. Bhishma Narayan Singh and Deputy Minister Sh. Mohammad Usman Arif. One petitioner society and respondent society requested the Central Government in 1981 for allotment of land in South Delhi. They were informed of the ban and directed to approach DDA for allotment of land elsewhere.

Rajiv Gandhi became the 6th Prime Minister of India from 31.10.1984 to 1989. He took office after the 1984 assassination of his mother, Prime Minister Indira Gandhi, he became the youngest Indian Prime Minister at the age of 40. In December, the Congress party won the largest Lok Sabha majority to date, 411 seats out of 542. Sh. Abdul Ghafoor was made Minister of Urban Development who took charge on 31.12.1984.

Sh. Rajiv Gandhi's period in office was mired in controversies; perhaps the greatest crises were the Bhopal disaster, Bofors scandal. In mid-1987, the Bofors scandal damaged his corruption-free image and resulted in a major defeat for his party in the 1989 election.

The prime land of 72 acres, in the heart of South Delhi, covering part of Andrews Ganj, and earlier Aliganj named as Pinjrapole land, was eyed by all the politicians, bureaucrats, and business houses from 1985 and onwards. The land was evicted after 1985 when several developments had taken place in Delhi.

Harkishan Lal Kapoor was Chairman of DDA and Lieutenant Governor of Delhi from November 1985 until August 1988. Kapoor joined Indian National Congress after retirement from Indian Air Force. He was nominated for Rajya Sabha in 1985. He took oath on 3 January 1985 but resigned on 14 November 1985 to become Lieutenant Governor of Delhi. Kapur died at the age of 96 years on 14 February 2020 after a prolonged illness at Dehradun where he was residing with his daughter at her house on Rajpura Road. His cremation took place in the same evening with full honor at Lakhibagh Ghat.

Shri Abdul Ghafoor, the Minister of Housing and Urban Development, a Member of the Eighth, Tenth, and Twelfth Lok Sabhas from 1984 to 1989, 1991 to 1996, and 1998 to 1999. He represented the Siwan Parliamentary Constituency of Bihar during the Eighth Lok Sabha and the Gopalganj Constituency of the same State in the Tenth and Twelfth Lok Sabhas. He participated in the freedom struggle and suffered imprisonment during the 'Quit India Movement in 1942. Shri Abdul Ghafoor passed away at the age of 86 on 10tJuly 2004 at Patna, Bihar.

The dapper DDA Vice-Chairman Prem Kumar had run the sprawling DDA Empire like his personal kingdom for three years from 1983 to 1986. DDA was not developing its commercial complexes in west and east Delhi because of pressures from builders who were interested in keeping commercial building prices at a high rate due to the artificial scarcity of commercial space.

The Registrar of Cooperative Societies issued a notification in 1983 inviting applications for registration from cooperative societies for allotment of land. Two thousand and nine cooperative societies applied and the Registrar registered about 1500 societies in 1983. Around the same time, some cooperative societies were formed with Ministers and MP.S. as its members. They made direct applications to the current Works and Housing Minister, Sh. Abdul Ghafoor for allotment of land in South Delhi.

A cooperative housing society is a membership-based legal entity made of one or more residential buildings. To become a member, you must buy shares in the housing cooperative. In return, as a member, you get the right to occupy a housing unit in the society. These societies are formed to provide residential houses to their members. They purchase land, develop it, and construct houses or flats and allot the same two members. Some societies also provide loans at low rates of interest to members to construct their own houses.

On 15.10.1984, the Land and Development Office informed the Works and Housing Ministry that there was no land available in South Delhi, and whatever chunks of land were available were to be utilized for the general pool requirement of the Central Government employees. It was also clarified that the Land and Development Department only allot lands to institutions and not to any individuals or cooperative societies. On 13.11.1984, the DDA also informed the Ministry that no land was available in South Delhi. They were also informed that about 2000 acres of land would be available in West Delhi by March 1985.

The Central Government had leased out about 70 acres of land between Andrews Ganj and Sadiq Nagar in south Delhi to Pinjrapole Society. Their lease was terminated, and an eviction order was initiated under the Public Premises Act passed against the Society on 23.9.83. The order was challenged by the Society in Delhi High Court. A learned Single Judge of this

Court dismissed the writ petition. The Society had filed a special leave petition in Supreme Court (SLP No. 9103/1984). In the said Special Leave Petition, a counter-affidavit was filed on behalf of the Union of India in October 1984. The Government of India pleaded before the Supreme Court:

"The Union of India is in urgent need of the land which is situated amid the city behind Andrews Ganj for construction of General Pool Staff Quarters and other public buildings."

The Supreme Court dismissed the Special Leave Petition and directed that the land in question be handed over to the Central Government on or before 30.05.1985. The Central Government then took possession on 30.05.1985.

# Chapter: Nine

*Andrews Ganj Land Allotted to Member of Parliament Society's by Congress Government*

After the Supreme Court dismissed the Special Leave Petition of Pinjrapole Society, the then Minister for Works and Housing (Urban Development) decided to allow the said land in South Delhi principally to the Cooperative Societies of which the Ministers and M. Ps. were the members. On 9.3.1985, the Minister made allotment of land to five such Cooperative Societies. Originally, the proposal was to hand over the said land to the DDA.; however, it was decided the land should not be entrusted to the DDA, and instead, the L&D.O. should make the allotment itself.

The allotment to five cooperative societies was made on 9.3.1985 without formally superseding the Ministerial decision taken in 1961, and the ban on allotment imposed in 1972 and 1981. After the initial allotment to five societies, the allotment was made to four more societies. Three of them consisted of M.P.S. as members. One society was formed by officers and employees of the Works and Housing Ministry.

The intent to grab material benefits and lands was so widespread that it paralyzed legal processes and norms of private and public morality, especially Andrews Ganj land being the most prime land in South Delhi. No section of society is free from it. The real question raised by the Supreme Court was whether the scam involved somebody being declined the land under the favoritism act? About 27 acres of the prime land of Andrews Ganj had been allotted by the Minister of Housing and Urban Development, Sh. Abdul Ghafoor and the Secretary, Sh. Romesh Sharma, was it favoritism? This land was allotted to nine Cooperative Group Housing Societies on 31.3.1986 hurriedly without giving opportunities to other societies.

A secretary to the Government of India is the administrative head of a ministry or department and is the principal adviser to the minister in charge on all matters of policy and administration. The responsibility in this regard is complete and undivided. Secretaries report to their ministerial cabinet minister and the prime minister.

The joint secretary is in charge of the necessary measure of independent functionality of the department allocated and entrusted to him. Additional secretaries and joint secretaries are responsible for filing all affidavits and responses before the Supreme Court of India.

As regards the price of land, a reference was made to the Finance Ministry. They pointed out the prices of land in South Delhi were fixed between Rs. 1200.00 (US Dollar 138.56) to Rs. 2000.00 (US Dollar 231) per square yard in 1981 and considering the steep increase in Delhi was necessary to re-determine market rates of land all over. The Finance Ministry also suggested that rates of land should be allotted to cooperative societies by revising past regulations to widen the gap between such rates and the market value.

The Ministry also suggested unearned income on the sale of the land by the allottee should be collected at the beginning. The Ministry was, however, persuaded by reference to the DDA prices that the proper rate for the said cooperative societies would be Rs. 474.00 (US Dollar 54.73) per sq. yard. Thereafter, the Works and Housing Ministry fixed Rs. 474.00 (US Dollar

54.73) per sq. yard as the rate for allotment to the said societies.

The final notification for allotment was set on the land to nine respondent cooperative societies issued on 31.3.1986. The 70 acres of land layout plan bears the same date, viz. 31.3.1986. The allotment was communicated to individual societies on 2.4.1986. On 4.4.1986, the 1972 ban on allotment of land in South Delhi was withdrawn by formal order. Between 8 to 10 days, the societies made the payments for the land and by 15.4.1986, possession of the land was given to almost all Societies.

To complete the scam within a short period of about eight to ten days, the allotment letters were sent, the premium amount was paid, and physical possession was given to the Societies. Many other applicants were neglected. The allotments made mala fides, favoritism, and abuse of authority in favor of Ministers, ex-Ministers, Members of Parliament., their relatives, and high Government officials belonging to the Ministry of Works & Housing, and Ministry of Urban Development. While allotting the land, no norms or guidelines were followed. The allotments were arbitrary, illegal, and vocative resulting in the scam of Andrews Ganj.

The entire plan of 72 acres of prime land at Pinjrapole Andrews Ganj was sabotaged by the Congress Ministers allotting the land to certain Group Housing Societies namely:

| S.No. | Name of Society | No. of Members | Extent |
|---|---|---|---|
| 1 | Nav Sansad Vihar Co-operative Group Housing Society | 300 | 5.00 acres |
| 2 | Jawaharlal Co-operative Group Housing Society | 132 | 2.20 acres |
| 3 | Fakruddin Memorial Co-operative Group Housing Society | 210 | 4.00 acres |
| 4 | Sriketan Co-operative Group Housing Society | 180 | 3.00 acres |
| 5 | Hum Sub Co-operative Group Housing Society | 150 | 2.50 acres |

| | | | |
|---|---|---|---|
| 6 | Neelanchai Co-operative Group Housing Society | 90 | 1.50 acres |
| 7 | Sansad Vihar Co-operative Group Housing Society | 135 | 2.25 acres |
| 8 | Dakshina Co-operative Group Housing Society | 259 | 4.30 acres |
| 9 | Priyadarshini Co-operative Group Housing Society | 135 | 2.25 acres |
| | | Total | 27 acres |

# Chapter: Ten

*Still 43 Acres of Andrews Ganj Land Was Proposed to Be Misused*

After the first scam began in 1950 and extended to 1985, the Andrews Ganj land measured 72 acres. Now, the second scam of Andrews Ganj land started after the above allotments to a Member of Parliament and Government officers owning these Co-operative Societies directly or indirectly. In order for an allotment of land to the societies, there had to be certain accepted norms such as "first come first served basis", "completion of formalities", such as a collection of affidavits, etc. But none of the above-listed items were followed before the grabbing of precious Andrews Ganj land.

The societies were not informed as to what norm is being followed for allotment of the land in question. It was intended to follow the principle of "first come first served". The said norm was also not disclosed to the public at large. The allotment of the land to the societies on the principle of first come first served also was not universally applied to all the societies who had been allotted land. There was no rationale behind these allotments and the public interest was relegated to a secondary position in the decision making.

It was unknown to the Minister as to who the members of cooperative societies were while making the allotment. Only one fact remained clear: these people were Members of Parliament. After the land was allotted, the Land and Development Officer was directed to obtain the lists of members in the various cooperative societies. It was made mandatory in the allotment letters that the societies shall furnish lists of the members duly certified by the Registrar, Cooperative Societies.

It was never justified how the land was earmarked for general pool housing and allotted to the cooperative societies of M.P.S., nor the cooperative society officials of the Urban Development Ministry. The Ministry filed a solemn affidavit before the Supreme Court in SLP. There was no 9103/1984 stating the urgent need for land for the construction of general pool staff quarters and other public buildings.

As my quest continued, I found myself turning up more questions than answers. For example, how could a representation (in the form of a decision) made to the Supreme Court be side-lined between the dismissal of the Special Leave Petition by the Supreme Court and getting the actual possession of the land from the Pinjrapole Society? Or how could the utilization of land for public purposes be converted to the private residential requirements of a few cooperative societies?

The allotments were issued in violation of the sworn-in affidavit before the Supreme Court by the Ministry and allotments were detrimental to public interest resulting in the second scam of the Andrews Ganj land. In question are thus hit by the principle of estoppel and detriment to the public interest. Still, the proposal of the 43-acre land balance was proposed to be utilized for General Pool Housing, justifying the nine allotments of 27 acres allotted to the societies.

The layout plan submitted for these 43 acres was different as the entire land was not proposed to be utilized for general pool housing as excluding Community centers, neighborhood parks, roads, etc. The general pool housing would not have more than 17 to 18 acres. In essence, this fact further aggravated the scam of Andrews Ganj land.

The further scam was committed by fixing the land price arbitrarily at Rs. 474.00 (US Dollar 37.61) per sq. yard. This was justified by the officers of the Ministry because of the low price on a no-profit, the no-loss basis is charged for encouraging cooperative group housing societies considered at a subsidized price. The Finance Ministry stated that the unofficial figure of the market price in South Delhi is about Rs. six thousand (US Dollar 476.19) per sq. yard. The initial object of large-scale acquisition of land in Delhi was to arrest speculation in the land prices.

In my findings, this information made no sense. The DDA as the Government agency itself had largely contributed to rocketing prices through its method of selective auctioning of land in Delhi. The DDA had also fixed rates of lands in different areas to mop up unearned income on the sales of land. In South Delhi areas, Rs. 4,000.00 (US Dollar 317.46) per sq. yard was fixed by the DDA as the notional price of land. In the face of these hard facts, what was the rational justification for giving land to cooperative societies at a 1/15th price of the market value? Was it not a scam?

As the additional population increases in Delhi every year, scarcity of land was being aggravated year to year. As a policy, DDA was not allotting plots of land to a single holder, but only to group housing societies. An ordinary resident who could not become a member of society had little to no buying power compared to a member of the society. The price difference was like 1/15 the which resulted in discrimination. without any rationale or basis, the allotments to these societies even if cooperative societies being run on no profit no loss could not be treated as a separate class causing such huge loss to the public exchequer which resulted in a Scam.

If 50 big industrialists come together and form a cooperative housing society, would it be justified to give them land at a subsidized price on a no-profit, no-loss basis? Merely being a cooperative society was not a rational criterion of classification on forgiving valuable lands in South Delhi, for almost a song. It was justified that the land is given to cooperative societies and not using it for general pool housing. As the ministry has a shortage of funds for general pool constructions of the houses for Government officers.

The idea itself is contrary when the land was sold at 1/15th of the market price.

The Finance Ministry also suggested selling at the market price which was caved in at a subsequent stage without any rational reason. Not to mention, the allotment of the lands to these nine Cooperative Societies for Rs. 474.00 (US Dollar 37.61) per sq. yard was arbitrary and showed the big scam. The allotment of 27 acres resulted in a loss to the Government exchequer of Rs. 25 crores (US Dollar 1.98 crore) in 1986, which was a big value.

# Chapter: Eleven

*Justification by Congress Government of The Allotment of Andrews Ganj Land*

The files disclosed by the erstwhile Minister showed only the cooperative societies Members of Parliament. At no time did he explain the decision for making allotments of this prime land in South Delhi.

In fact, the Minister had asked the cooperative societies to provide a breakdown of membership including the Members of Parliament. The officials of the Ministry had, however, cautioned that if the allotment was made wholly, it would become discriminatory. Therefore, the membership number was increased in some societies to include non-Members of Parliament.

In some societies, relatives of Parliament were accepted as additional members, so it did not appear to be Members of Parliament society. Even if the Society of Members of Parliament is treated at par with societies of professionals like lawyers and journalists some rational principles are required to be followed for such schemes but in this case, it apparently appeared to be deliberate, intentional resulting in the Scam of Andrews Ganj land.

The question that arises is how could the land be allotted at subsidized rates to six or seven cooperative societies of Member of Parliament, while there are only one or two societies of one class of professionals?

In my recent finding, it gnawed at me to learn how the relatives of Parliament could be clubbed with the Member of Parliament? Or why should the relatives be treated favorably over the other residents of Delhi?

The scam brought clarity as time passed, so why should the non-resident Members of Parliament be preferred over the permanent residents of Delhi? They are the ones in dire need of housing sites. My questions continued as to why the Members of Parliament did want to settle in Delhi given special treatment at the cost of other citizens who wished to be permanent residents of Delhi? Is it not a scam?

It was clear from the file that even in the class of cooperative societies of Members of Parliament there is no equal treatment. The Registrar of Cooperative Societies also adopted different criteria, while issuing registration certificates. For some, the certificate was issued without final verification of membership and other formalities, and the names were forwarded to the Central Government and DDA. While in other cases, registration certificates were delayed for verification of membership and completion of certain formalities. Was it not a scam?

Two society officials in Urban Development Ministry proper and the Land & Development Office both applied for allotment in 1981 in South Delhi. They were directed to make applications to DDA because there was a ban on the allotment in South Delhi. Both societies were allotted lands by the DDA in other parts of Delhi and had taken possession of the land in West Delhi.

When these two societies found that lands were being allotted to Cooperative Societies in South Delhi, both the societies again applied for land in South Delhi instead of land allotted to them. The cooperative society of the officials of Urban Development Ministry proper got the allotment in South Delhi while the others could not. It was said the land is already allotted to it in other parts of Delhi.

Normally, allotment by DDA prohibits transfers for the first ten years. But in these nine allotments, the terms and conditions of Andrews Ganj land had no such restriction or bar stipulation. The allottee could make a huge profit by selling the land/flats which were again on favors granted.

# Chapter: Twelve

*Prabhu Chawla, An Eminent Journalist*

Prabhu Chawla, a journalist, was the editorial director of the New Indian Express. But before his assignment with The New Indian Express, he was the editor of Language Publications in India Today news magazine. However, before holding this post, he worked as the group editorial director of India Today Group until November 2010. Mr. Chawla has the unique distinction of being the only journalist in India whose story had led to the fall of a Government in New Delhi.

Prabhu Chawla scooped the controversial Jain Commission report on the assassination of Rajiv Gandhi. Its publication in the magazine led to Congress withdrawing support to the United Front Government, which led to the fall of the Inder Kumar Gujral-led regime in 1997. While in India Today, he hosted a popular talk show called *Seedhi Baat* on the Aaj Tak channel where he grilled prominent personalities. But after leaving the group, he was replaced by M. J. Akbar.

Prabhu Chawla is one of the top talk show hosts in India and his weekly show, *Teekhi Baat* on the IBN7 channel, had one of the highest ratings for a news-based program. Currently, he is hosting *Sachchi Baat* on National Voice, *Siddhi Gal* on PTC News, and is the editorial director of The New Indian Express Group. Currently, Prabhu Chawla has his own YouTube channel.

Prabhu Chawla did an article against Sh. Prem Kumar on 15 July 1986 in India Today with the heading:

*DDA vice-chairman Prem Kumar asked to quit, faces scandalous land deals, housing charges.*

As meteoric as his rise to the prestigious post of the Delhi Development Authority's vice-chairmanship was his sudden and ignominious exit last month, wreathed in the shroud of scandal. For the last three years, the dapper Prem Kumar had run the sprawling DDA Empire like his personal kingdom.

Sourced from this news, one of the societies, Vikas Vihar Co-operative Group Housing Society Ltd. was not allotted the Andrews Ganj land. He then filed Civil Writ Petition before the High Court of Delhi against the Government through the Ministry of

Urban Development and against the nine societies as well as the Land & Development Office and DDA. The battery of lawyers appeared: R.S. Narula, D.S. Narula, S.P. Singh, N.S. Vashisth, R.K. Anand, S.P. Sharma, Kapil Sibal, Y.R. Chitley, U.R. Lalit, K.N. Bhatt, V.P. Singh, Badan Durreji, Arjun Bhandari and M.C. Bhandare, Advs.

The Division Bench of the High Court of Delhi decided on 1 June 1987, by R.N. Aggarwal and S.B. Wad, JJ, that the case quashing all the nine allotments indirectly be observed as a scam:

"Our task in these writ petitions is rendered easier by the Union of India admitting through its counter-affidavit that no norms or guidelines were followed while making the impugned allotments. In these days of rumors and alleged scandals, the fourth nightstand taken by the Union of India is singularly welcome. Admission of a mistake creates hope for the future. It has the freshness of Rajnigandha as the name of one of the petitioner societies suggests.

"But this is not an excuse for ignoring the legitimate grievances. A solution must be attempted within the confines of the law. We must prevent arbitrariness in executive actions and transgression of the law. Since the Union of India has partially conceded the petitioners' claim on this count, we need not go to the other pleas of the petitioners."

On a consideration of the relevant cases cited at the bar, the following propositions may be taken as well established:

State-owned or public-owned property is not to be dealt with at the absolute discretion of the executive. Certain precepts must be observed because public interest is the paramount consideration. One method of securing the public interest that is considered necessary when disposing of a property is to sell the property by public auction or by inviting tenders. Though that is the ordinary rule, it is not an invariable rule.

There may be situations where there are compelling reasons for necessitating departure from the rule, but then the reasons for the departure must be rational and should not be suggestive of discrimination. The appearance of public justice is as important as doing justice. Nothing should be done which gives an appearance of bias, jobbery, or nepotism.

If the land in question was entrusted to the DDA and if they make the allotment; the normal condition of the lease would have applied to the respondent societies. Otherwise, the allotments suffer from many infirmities; therefore, no one is inclined to give exclusive relief to some societies.

We realize that the problem is too complex and stupendous for any Government to resolve. But if some rational norms are laid down by the Government, and are uniformly and impartially followed, the problem can be satisfactorily tackled. Instead of Judges taking over the functions of an administrator, it is more fruitful if the administrator follows judicial methods of objectivity and impartiality.

The allotment of lands to respondent societies suffers from arbitrariness and is violative of Article 14 of the Constitution. The impugned order dated 31.3.1986 and the individual allotments dated 2.4.1986 are set aside. The Union of India should seriously reconsider whether the land in question should be allotted to the co-operative societies or whether the land should be reserved for the general pool staff housing. The government has accepted legal infirmity in the initial allotment. The Union of India should take back the possession immediately.

# Chapter: Thirteen

*DDA vice-chairman Prem Kumar*

DDA vice-chairman Prem Kumar was asked to quit after facing scandalous land deals and housing charges. But three weeks before his term was to expire, Kumar was faced with the added humiliation of having CBI sleuths crawling all over his house searching for proof of connections between him and the numerous, scandalous land deals and award of lucrative housing construction contracts to a clutch of favored contractors during his tenure.

J.K. Varshney was also removed, along with DDA's engineer member and one of his closest colleagues in the organization, who were also raided by the CBI. After the raids, the CBI registered a case against both under Section 5 (2) 5 (1) D for the Prevention of Corruption Act which deals with the "abuse of official position to cause pecuniary advantage to self or others."

Though both Kumar and Varshney were tight-lipped, the crackdown followed a flurry of corruption charges recently leveled against them by Members of Parliament and Delhi's Metropolitan Council. A note submitted to the prime minister by a group of 16 MPs on June 3 demanded that a thorough inquiry by the CBI should be held into the frauds committed by the DDA.

The memorandum accused Kumar and Varshney of awarding house building contracts worth over Rs 140 crore to those whose incapacity to carry out the projects was known to the DDA. The allotment of prized South Delhi flats was given to their friends and relatives. Also, the delay in recovery of dues worth over Rs 40 crore from leading builders of Delhi permitted the construction of a commercial complex on green belt land.

Besides the BJP, the opposition party at the relevant time had also submitted a detailed charge-sheet to the prime minister listing specific cases of substandard houses, incomplete sewage works for which payments had already been made, and leakage of highly confidential New Delhi Master Plans to selected builders and land developers. They listed instances when, for example, the DDA engineer member delayed clearing the file containing designs for the development of a 200-acre Bhola Nath Nagar

Commercial Complex in Shahdara. The delay lasted for over a year because it would have led to a drop in commercial space prices.

The DDA even ignored written instructions from Delhi's Lt. Governor H.L. Kapoor to expedite the development of commercial land in Delhi.

The memo charged that it was solely due to connivance between the DDA and certain builders that commercial land prices in Delhi have soared by over 200 percent during the last three years. While three commercial estates were developed earlier, not one was developed during Kumar's tenure. The allegations appeared to be somewhat substantiated by the fact that among the documents recovered by the CBI during their raid on the premises of prominent builders in the city were confidential DDA files.

Madan Lal Khurana, president of the Delhi unit of the BJP, stated: "The DDA was giving favor to property dealers who in turn were sharing their profits with DDA officials."

But ultimately, it was Kumar's proximity to a clique of politicians and civil servants that proved his biggest liability. Believing himself insured by the support of his friends in South Block, he openly defied the Lt. Governor, who is also the chairman of the DDA. He refused to accompany Kapoor on his visits to various localities and turned a deaf ear when questioned on his claims about the construction of over a lakh houses and removal of corrupt officials.

But Kapoor was made of sterner stuff than Kumar imagined. Since Kapoor had made “Operation DDA clean-up” his prime objective, he compiled a confidential report on corruption in the DDA and sent it privately to the prime minister.

Kumar, however, managed to stave off any immediate action with the help of Urban Development Minister, Abdul Ghafoor and Ministry Secretary, Romesh Chandra, both of whom favored another extension for him. He also succeeded in getting his name recommended for the chairmanship of Air India, which was scuttled at the last moment by Minister of State for Civil Aviation, Jagdish Tytler. But this only made the Lt. Governor more determined to bring Kumar to book.

Kapoor personally met the prime minister and reportedly told him that the Government's image would be badly damaged if Kumar continued. Soon after, Ghafoor received instructions to send Kumar and Varshney on leave, pending investigations.

After having won his moral victory, Kapoor accelerated his plans for cleaning up the controversial organization.

He stated, “We want to make the DDA a live and responsive organization, and not to work against the interest of those whom it is expected to serve.” Not to mention the interests of those who served.

# Chapter: Fourteen

*Interference of Prime Minister for The Land*

As the pending litigation waned before the High Court, the scam continued for the balance of 72 acres.

Sh. M.B. Sexana, Senior Architect, CPWD vide letter dated 25.7.1986 to the Secretary, DUAC submitted:

"The layout plan for 70.43 acres of land at Pinjrapole was initially submitted to Delhi Urban Art Commission in March 1985 for approval at the concept stage.

"Since then, the requirements have changed in the instance of the Government of India. Accordingly, a revised layout plan drawing No. TP-3109 in quadruplicate with the following documents are submitted for Commission consideration.

1. Drawing No. TP 3109 - 2 copies
2. Model of layout
3. Photographs of site brief report.

The Ministry of Urban Development is pressing hard for early finalization. It is, therefore, requested the layout plan be put before the Commission.

The submissions of Sh. M.B. Sexana were countered by Sh. J.J.S. Majithia, Assistant Secretary

(Tech.), DUAC vide letter dated 29.7.1986 to the Senior Architect, CPWD as follows:

"In order to enable us to scrutinize the project properly, I am directed to request you to submit the following information/material:

i. Copy of the zonal plan, along with them its reports.
ii. Density prescribed for the areas as per zonal plan and not densities for various pockets.
iii. Modifications made in the layout plan from the zonal plan, if any.
iv. Structure plan of the total complex indicating the facilities provide W.R.T., the requirements of the zonal plan.
v. Set-back lines /envelope control in the various plots with height restrictions.
vi. Urban, along with the block model and its photographs (8"x10").
vii. Site photographs (8" x10")
viii. A detailed report indicating the approach of development and the salient features of the scheme.

ix. Two copies of the layout plan and any other drawing required to explain the proposal.

x. Any other material which would help the Commission to understand the concept of development."

The above information was sought in ten days from CPWD, Ministry of Works & Housing.

On 2.9.1986, DDA Vice-Chairman, Sh. Om Kumar reported to the Secretary, Smt. Sarla Grewal, Prime Minister of India's office said that as per telephonic conversation, the change of land use from the agricultural green belt is submitted herewith to the locational plan for consideration, perusal, and approval. Various ministries, including the office of Prime Minister of India, continued to interfere to grape the precious Andrews Ganj land. The Railway Ministry for its freight operation computer complex also requested the use of this land.

A letter dated 26.9.1986 was written by the Prime Minister of India through Joint Secretary Sh. Wajahat Habibullah to Sh. Om Kumar, DDA Vice-Chairman informing them that the land could be allotted for Indira Gandhi National open university. The area is shown in Delhi Master Plan, 1962 was a green belt and is now indicated as recreational in the draft plan, 2001. On the other side, the Ministry of External Affairs was also interested in this land for its Foreign Service training institute. The Sports Authority through the Sports Ministry also tried to get this land for Afro Asian Games in 1991.

Shri Wajahat Habibullah, Joint Secretary, Prime Minister's Office through a letter dated 26 September 1986 to Shri Om Kumar, Vice Chairman, DDA kindly refer to the D.O. No. DA/VC/86/222 dated 3 September 1986 to the Secretary to the Prime Minister regarding urgent proposals for change on land use in four cases. The matter was put up to the Prime Minister who has desired these four cases may be rejected.

# Chapter: Fifteen

*Scam of Andrews Ganj Land Continued*

The files kept shuttling from one department to the other for approval of the layout plan. It went on for various clarification from 1985 to 1988. Minister Abdul Ghafoor was shunted out on 22.10.1986 and Smt. Mohsina Kidwai was made the Minister of Urban Development on 22.10.1986 by Prime Minister Sh. Rajiv Gandhi remained the minister until 2.12.1989 when Sh. Rajiv Gandhi Government resigned for elections.

It was submitted again by Sh. M.B. Sexana, Senior Architect, CPWD vide letter dated 29.4.1988 to the Secretary, DUAC as follows:

"A total of 73.43 acres of land is available at Pinjrapole near Andrews Ganj. Out of this total plan, part of the land is air marked for General Pool Housing along with one Community/Shopping Centre, and the rest of the land was earmarked for various group housing societies.

"As per the recent management of committee meeting held in the chamber of the Secretary, Ministry of Urban Development, it was decided that conceptual approval from the Urban Art Commission concerning pocket 'B' measuring 8 acres meant for General Pool housing may be taken accordingly. The following set of drawings have been prepared in this office, which is submitted to the Commission for their conceptual approval.

"Overall layout plan drawing No. TP-3180 along with the model and two photographs of the same Detail layout plan of pocket 'B' drawing No. TP-3179 along with model and photographs of the same. The Block model of the Shopping-cum-Community Center has also been incorporated in the overall layout model and layout plan mentioned above. Type V 8 storied building plans drawing No. SAI/1008-1013. Type VI 12 storied building drawing No. SAI/920, 1016-1019. Proposed urban form for Community Center at Pinjrapole drawing No. TP-3197. Set of photographs showing the environment of the area and the neighboring areas."

It is requested that the scheme be submitted before the Commission for approval. In reply to the above, Sh. Iqbal Singh, Architect Secretary, and CPWD vide letter dated 9.5.1988 to The Secretary, DUAC as follows:

"Overall layout plan drawing No. TP-3180 along with the model. Detail layout plan of pocket 'B' drawing No. TP-3179 along with the model. Type V 8 storied building plans drawing No. SAI/1008-1013. Type VI 12 storied building drawing No. SAI/920, 1016-1019 and SA (1) 920. Proposed urban form for Community Center drawing No. TP-3197. Set of photographs showing the environment of the area."

Further, Sh. Iqbal Singh, Architect Secretary, CPWD vide letter dated 11.5.1988 to The Secretary, DUAC as follows:

"In continuation of a letter dated 9.5.88, the model photographs 5 Nos. for perusal was submitted."

The Jt. Secretary Shri Desh Raj Singh of the Ministry in Urban Development took up the meeting in the Chamber of the Secretary. The proposal was for 15 acres out of 73 at Pinjrapole. It was decided by DUAC that the scheme should be developed on principles of a sound and comprehensive integrated concept of development rather than adopting a piecemeal approach. It should be ensured that this concept is not pre-empted by arbitrary divisions of the overall pockets of land, or by allotment of individual plots. DUAC did not approve because the use did not conform as prescribed in the Zonal Development Plan. DUAC did not approve because the use of land does not conform as prescribed in the Zonal Development Plan.

# Chapter: Sixteen

*Layout Plans Rejected by DUAC At Conceptual Stage Itself*

The proposal, as submitted by the Ministry of Works & Housing, was considered by the Delhi Urban Art Commission, but rejected as decided in the minutes at the 545th meeting of the Delhi Urban Art Commission held on May 20, 1988.

General Pool Housing at Pinjrapole (conceptual stage), it was observed:

The above-mentioned proposal, as directly submitted by the Senior Architect, CPWD, was examined and discussed with him. It was noted that the Senior Architect prepared the proposal for only a small pocket of 8 acres in addition to the community center, including another 7 acres out of the total land measuring about 73 acres at Pinjrapole. After deliberations, the following observations were made:

The proposal did not seem to respect the area and configuration of the zonal green as shown in the zonal plan of the area. Nor did the piecemeal approach adopt the developing isolated pockets conducive to the concept of comprehensive integrated development. The demarcation of plots that were earmarked for a different group in the housing schemes was found within the overall housing development. The plan seemed to be on an arbitrary basis without any regard to the open space system, traffic circulation system, and various components required for the proposed development over such a large area.

The internal road connecting two major traffic arteries of the city on the east and west boundaries is likely to encourage more through traffic, which would not be desirable. One essential consideration on the points of entry to the plot should be carefully chosen while keeping in view the traffic on the major artery, road junctions, and the adjoining fly-over, etc. If the density is not adopted properly for the various housing groups, components in the plot should be rationalized in consultation with the DDA. Not to mention, the proposal of the community center should be adequately detailed and properly integrated into the overall scheme.

The scheme should be developed on principles of a sound, comprehensive and integrated concept of development rather than adopting a piecemeal approach, and it should be ensured that this concept is not pre-empted by arbitrary divisions of the overall pockets of land, or by allotment of individual plots.

All the members present concur to the above and sent back an amended proposal to the Ministry communicating the rejection along with another letter dated 3.6.1988 written by Sh. J.J.S. Majithia, Secretary (Tech.), DUAC.

In this period, in August 1988, Pavan Sachdeva's wife gave birth to a third daughter. But he remained very busy while progressing in his export business. He could hardly devote any time to home as he was too busy making money and establishing his legitimate growth.

In pursuance of the rejection of the proposal of Andrews Ganj, a meeting was held in the office room of Shri R.K. Thakkar; an additional Secretary entered at 4:00 p.m. on 21 December 1988 to consider the question of preparation on the layout plan for the proposed land in Pinjrapole. It was to be utilized for the construction of residential accommodation in the General Pool. All the officers of the Ministry, CPWD, and the Secretary of the DUAC were present in this meeting and it was concluded that:

At the outset, it was explained that there were about 73 acres of land belonging to the Government in Pinjrapole, New Delhi; the land use was to be dedicated to residential use. Originally, the entire land, minus 8 acres earmarked for community facilities for the Sub-District, was proposed to be utilized for the construction of general pool accommodation. The CPWD had, accordingly, prepared a draft layout plan for the area, proposing the construction of general pool quarters of different types (Types I to VI) and other necessary community facilities like parks, toilets, primary schools, electric substations, etc.

The layout plan had been submitted to the DUAC who, however, refused the plan as prescribed in the zonal development, particularly regarding the green area. DUAC had also made some other observations on this layout plan.

In the meantime, the Government allotted about 27 acres for general pool accommodation to 9 Group Housing Cooperative Societies.

# Chapter: Seventeen

*High Court Held Allotments of Andrews Ganj Illegal*

On quashing the nine allotments on 1 June 1987 by the High Court of Delhi, the aggrieved nine societies went to the Supreme Court. They filed Civil Appeals, which were decided on 5 April 1989. The scam again kept the Andrews Ganj' precious land in abeyance without any development in the hands of the Ministry of Urban Development, all leading to the continuous scam.

During the meeting, the Ministry observed the allotment of 27 acres had since been set aside by the Delhi High Court. The same of the affected Group Housing Societies had filed an appeal (SLP) against the decision of the High Court in the Supreme Court. While admitting the SLP, the Supreme Court passed an interim order directing the nature of land in dispute that should not, in any way, be altered until the final decision on the SLP. It had, therefore, been decided to only utilize the undisputed land for the construction of general pool accommodation.

The CPWD had accordingly planned the construction of 224 Type V quarters and 56 Type VI quarters on this land, along with administrative approval and expenditure sanction for 63 Type V and the Government had also issued 33 types, VI of which. It had also been decided that the Chief Architect, CPWD, would prepare a layout plan only for the undisputed portion of land affected by the interim order of the Supreme Court, and then get the same approval by the DUAC.

Once they achieved the approval, the Chief Architect proposed a layout plan. The important ones did not respect the area and configuration of the zonal green as shown in the zonal department plan. The demarcation for different group housing societies appeared to have been one of an arbitrary decision without regard to the open space system, traffic circulation system, and various components required for the proposed development over such a large area.

The DUAC also made observations concerning the proposed internal road. As an example, the point of entry, the density, and proposal of the Community Center. They desired the scheme to be developed on principles of a sound comprehensive and integrated concept of development rather than adopting a piecemeal approach. This was to ensure the concept was not prompted by arbitrary divisions of the overall pockets or by allotment of individual plots.

It was pointed out by the Senior Architect, CPWD that the density of population prescribed in this area as per the Zonal Development Plan was 100 persons or 30 dwelling units per acre. The Group Housing Societies to whom 27 acres of land had been parcelled could, as per the letters of allotment, put up 60 dwelling units per acre, subject, of course, to their building plans being approved by the local bodies. It was possible that at the rate of 30 dwelling units per acre, the total number of dwelling units could be planned in the whole area minus 7 acres set up for the community centers.

Assuming the worst and supposing the Supreme Court verdict went in favor of Group Housing Societies, they would have to be permitted to put up 1,620 dwelling units on the gross area of 27 acres allotted to them. This would leave 330 dwelling units of different types which could be put up by the

Government in the general pool on the portion of land, which was not under dispute.

It was proposed that 270 quarters of different types could be constructed on the undisputed portion of land. TII would be no loss to the Government in terms of the number of quarters to be put up on this portion; even if the land allotted to the Societies were ultimately decided by the Supreme Court to be restored to them.

After considering all aspects of the matter, the following decisions were taken:

The Chief Architect, CPWD, would prepare two alternative layout plans for the 73 acres of land.

The first alternative plan would be on the assumption the area allotted to the group housing societies would be restored to them.

The second alternative plan would assume that the entire area, including the land earlier allotted to the Group Housing Societies, would be available for putting up residential accommodation in the general pool.

In both the alternative layout plans, the number and types of quarters constructed in the general pool, not under dispute—would be constant. The plan allows the CPWD to construct accommodations in the general pool, irrespective of the verdict by the Supreme Court on the disputed portion of land.

While preparing the two alternative layout plans, the Chief Architect, CPWD would keep in mind the planning at building controls regarding the green area, FAR, green coverage, the density of population, height, underground parking, etc. He would also keep in mind the observations made by the DUAC, a necessary liaison with the DDA for the planning of the Community Center.

There should be no objection to assuming suitable modifications allotted to different Group Housing Societies in the alternative layout plan No. 1. As long as their location is plotted on the total area under dispute.

Once the drafts of the two alternative layout plans had been prepared by the Chief Architect, these will be considered in a meeting held in the office room of

Additional Secretaries to which representatives of the DDA, besides those of the CPW, DUAC, NDMC/MCD, would be invited.

After approval of the two alternative plans by the Ministry, these would be presented by the Chief Architect to the DUAC with the necessary block models, etc., for approval. The meeting ended with a vote of thanks to the Chair.

# Chapter: Eighteen

*Justification by Supreme Court*

The Chief Justice Sh. R.S. Pathak and Justice S. Natarajan decided these bunch of SLPs on the arguments of eminent Lawyer Sh. R.K. Anand confirmed the order of the High Court of Delhi of quashing nine allotments of 27 acres of land out of 72 acres of land at Andrews Ganj, and the appeals of these nine societies were dismissed. It revealed a few more facts about the Andrews Ganj scam.

By an order made under the Allocation of Business Rules, the administration of these lands, which are properties of the Union, vests in the Ministry of Urban Development Land and Development Office. It is the field office of the Ministry of Urban Development to allot these lands under an order of the Ministry and administer the leases. Later, some of these Nazul lands were placed at the disposal of the Delhi Improvement Trust for constructing buildings allocated to the public by allotment or auction.

In the year 1957, the Delhi Development Act was passed. In terms of the Act, the Delhi Development Authority (short for the D.D.A.) was made up; the Delhi Improvement Trust was merged with the

D.D.A. After its formation, the D.D.A. acquired large areas of land in Delhi for development, and thereafter allotted or auctioned to the public on a lease-hold basis. In 1961, the Government of India formulated certain policies for governing the development and distribution/allotment of lands to various institutions and individuals. One of those policies was given priority to cooperative group housing societies for allotment of the land.

The Government also decided to discontinue the scheme of plotted development, and instead use the lands for flats in multi-storied buildings by the D.D.A., or allow cooperative group housing societies to develop the land. It was also decided that because of the scarcity of land in South Delhi, group housing societies would be allotted land in East and West Delhi, and not land in South Delhi for the time being, except to such societies for whom commitment was already made before 1972.

It was also decided that the rate of premium for land allotted to cooperative group housing societies would be higher in South Delhi than in East or West Delhi.

Another policy decision was taken while allotting land to the cooperative group housing societies; however, special care should be taken to ensure the societies are allotted lands nearest to the places of employment of their members. Sometime later, the Government took further note of the situation caused by the scarcity of land, particularly in the South Delhi area, and created an executive decision in 1972 to impose a temporary ban on further allotment of lands in the South Delhi area.

The temporary ban was relaxed in 1979, but even so, it became necessary to impose restrictions during the period 1980 to 1983 on the registration of new cooperative group housing societies. Since 1983, almost all the societies registered after 1981 had by and large been allotted lands. The ban on registration of co-operative group housing societies was lifted, and the Lt. Governor of Delhi made an announcement regarding the same in the newspapers on 17.7.83. Because of it, the registration of new cooperative societies was resumed, and numerous group housing societies applied for registration during the years 1983-84.

On March 5, 1984, the Government of India decided as per terms set out below regarding the allotment of lands to newly registered societies in the year 1983-84. 1) As almost all the old societies were allotted land, the cooperative group housing societies registered in 1983-84 may be allotted land in batches. 2) As the land in East and West Delhi is almost exhausted, land in other areas should be considered for allotment to newly registered co-operative group housing societies. 3) For purposes of allotment, the seniority of registration is of no relevance. The Registrar, Cooperative Societies, should publish a notice calling the registered co-operative group housing societies, who have completed all formalities, to apply for allotment of land. The land should be allotted to societies on a first-come-first-served basis.

According to the above decision taken by the Government, the Registrar, Cooperative Societies[4] issued a notice in the newspapers on March 10, 1984, being directive under Rule 77 of Delhi Cooperative Societies Rules, 1973. Thereafter, on March 12, 1984,

[4] (Hajare, 2020)

a notice was issued by the Registrar, Cooperative Societies, inviting applications from societies for allotment of land.

DDA has now intimated that they would now consider allotment of land to Group Housing Societies registered in 1983-84. Those societies who have closed their membership and desire to seek land through DDA are requested to submit their membership list and other documents to the office of the Registrar, Co-operative Societies on prescribed proforma available with the office from 20 March 1984 and onward. Sanat Kaul, Registrar, Cooperative Societies, Delhi Administration, Old Court Bldg., Parliament Street, New Delhi-1. DIP/Dept. 132/84.

A further notice came to be issued on March 20, 1984, by the Assistant Registrar, Co-operative Societies. The said notice after referring to the two earlier notices stipulated the following eligibility conditions/formalities:

Application for allotment by co-operative group housing societies registered in 1983-84 should be in the prescribed proforma.

Application (in the prescribed proforma) should be accompanied by a forwarding letter and affidavit to be signed by the President/Vice President/Secretary of the Society as per prescribed formats.

Affidavits of individual members not already supplied earlier also to be submitted.

The total membership of the societies should be in multiples of 15.

On submission of the list of members to the Registrar, the membership shall be frozen at that number (which may vary from 60 to 300 and be a multiple of 15). 6. 6. New membership is possible only against vacancies due to exclusion, transfer, or resignation.

The rationale in prescribing the total membership to be in multiples of 15 was to facilitate the allotment of land, following the norm of 1 acre of land for 60 members of a cooperative group housing society.

In response to this notification, many societies submitted their applications for allotment of land. The Registrar of Cooperative Societies prepared a seniority list of 15 cooperative societies that had submitted their applications on the 20th and 21st of March 1984 and forwarded the same on 23rd March 1984 to the Vice-Chairman, D.D.A. On 30.5.1985.

# Chapter: Nineteen

*Land Remained Unutilized until 1989 Due to Congress Government, and Thereafter MS Shoes Was Made Scapegoat*

The government took possession of 72 acres in Sadiq Nagar/Andrews Ganj, while South Delhi was under the occupation of the Delhi Pinjrapole Society and with whom the Government of India was locked in a long, drawn-out legal battle to recover possession of the land. In truth, there was no long-drawn-out litigation since the stay granted by the High Court of Delhi was vacated by Sh. B. Datta, the Government Pleader. The deposit of Rs. 25,000/- (US Dollar 3230/-) directed by High Court vide order dated 20.8.1973 in Civil Writ No. 773 of 1973 by Justice H.L. Anand could not be done by Society. Sh. B. Datta reported on 24.7.1974, being the Government Pleader, that there is no stay order in favor of Pinjrapole Society. Accordingly, the eviction proceedings started in 1978. It was a scam by the officers pending litigation. The property was not evicted deliberately and intentionally.

While taking possession of the 72 acres from the Pinjrapole Society, the Government had already relaxed the ban on the attachment of land in South Delhi, as per its decision dated 5 March 1984. The Government gave instructions to the Land and

Development Officer to allot 27 acres of land out of the 72 acres to 9 cooperative societies. It was in such circumstances the general order of allotment in favor of nine cooperative societies came to pass on March 31, 1986.

The Nazul land is in question; as the cooperative societies were not entitled to claim priority based on seniority of registration, as such seniority will have relevance only in the case of allotment by the D.D.A. In the case of Nazul, it was said to always be open for the Government to make allotments according to its discretion. In exercise of the Government's discretionary powers, allotment of land in South Delhi had been made to six societies on a group housing basis, viz. 1) Tara 2) Naviketan 3) Kalkaji Best Friend's 4) Press Association 5) Business and Professional Women and 6) the Yamuna. Besides, the Army Welfare Association had also been allotted land in Som Vihar at R.K. Puram.

Since 1983, several societies comprised of numerous Members of Parliament, ex-Members of Parliament, Legislatures, Government Servants, and Professionals and Journalists were seeking allotment of land and had also made applications directly to the Government. Those applications were examined, but no allotment could be made, as sufficient land was not then available in South Delhi. Since in the year 1983-84, a piece of land measuring about 70 acres became available in South Delhi. It was decided to allow a portion of this land to cooperative group housing societies.

Consequently, the Government viewed consideration of the applications sent by the cooperative societies directly, as well as to the Registrar. The allotment of land to the nine societies had been made after due consideration of all the facts over nearly two years.

In so far as a fixation on the price of land, it was stated the price should be a rate 3.5 times more than the rate fixed for lands in other parts of Delhi which were allotted to cooperative societies. The policy of the Government was to charge subsidized rates for land concerning cooperative societies to encourage group housing. But even then, the Government fixed a value higher by 3.5 times for the land in South

Delhi once they consulted with the financial advisor and the Ministry of Finance.

Soon after repossessing the Nazul land from the Pinjrapole Society, the Ministry of Works and Housing made an allotment of land on 9.3.85 to five co-operative societies, four of them being respondents in the writ petition. Many of the people involved were Ministers and Parliament members. Originally, the proposal was to ensure the land be given to the DDA for allotment, according to prescribed norms. But curiously, the proposal was given go-bye, and it was decided to have the allotment done by the Ministry itself.

After the initial allotment to five societies (one being excluded subsequently), three of them being societies in which Members of Parliament were a member, and one society consisted of officers and employees of the Works and Housing Ministry; a reference was made to the Finance Ministry regarding the fixation on the price of the land. Though the Finance Ministry pointed out the price of land was fixed between Rs. 1200/- (US Dollar 138.56) to Rs. 2000/- (US Dollar

231/-) per sq. yard in 1981. The Housing Ministry, after a purported reference to the DDA prices, fixed the rate at Rs. 474/- (US Dollar 54.73) per sq. yard. However, the notional price fixed by the DDA for land in the South Delhi area was Rs. 4000/- (US Dollar 461.90) per sq. yard.

Within two days, the individual orders were made in favor of nine societies, after the general order of allotment was made on the very same day, the layout plan was prepared for the 70 acres of land. It was on 4.4.1986; the ban imposed in 1972 in South Delhi was withdrawn by formal order. But even before that, the Ministry had passed allotment orders. In about 8 to 10 days, the societies had made full payment for the land by 15.4.86, so possession of the lands had been given to almost all the societies.

# Chapter: Twenty

*Supreme Court Directed Government to Refund the Amounts with Interest @12% Received Against the Allotment of Andrew Ganj Land*

The allotment to the housing societies ran counter to the standing taken by the Union of India before the Supreme Court in getting possession of land from the Pinjrapole Society. They urgently needed the land for the construction of general pool staff quarters and other public buildings. The nothing in the file indicated the Minister concerned was anxious to allot land only to those cooperative societies, which comprised several Members of Parliament, but were being cautioned by the officials of the Ministry. The membership of the concerned societies was increased to include some more Members of Parliament and some non-legislators to get over any criticism that may be leveled for allotment of land to the concerned societies. In the matter of allotment to the favored societies, one society was discriminated against and not allotted land.

The first criticism was justified by the Government. The D.D.A., after being constituted, was entrusted with the task of allotting land. The Government had not given up or waived its right to allot Nazul land to various institutions and cooperative societies. As such, the Government had not done anything unusual or illegal in allotting land to the societies through the Ministry of Urban Development, instead of through the D.D.A.

As regards the second criticism, it was justified by the Government that since a policy decision had been taken in 1983, the land in other areas including South Delhi should be considered for allotment to newly registered cooperative societies, ignoring the earlier ban order in South Delhi. It had become dreamingly lifted, and only a formal order for lifting the ban was necessary, and it came to be passed on 4.4.1986.

Because there was criticism of allotment proceedings being carried out with unseemly haste, the Government was further justified in its actions. It was submitted, and the question of allotment was under pending consideration for about two years, and only passing after mature consideration.

The grievance was expressed by some societies registered before 1983-84 that they were not favored with the allotment of land, while the societies registered later had been allotted land. The answer the Government never committed itself to was that the allotment of land would only be available to new societies after satisfying the claims of the older societies.

The arbitrariness was leveled under the principle of "first come first served", which was said to have been followed by the Government in allotting the land. However, it had not been made known to all the societies and came to be known only to some of the societies. It may be because the Government had decided on March 5, 1984, that seniority of registration would be of no relevance for allotment. The Registrar of Co-operative Societies should publish a notice calling for applications from Housing Societies on a "first come, first served" basis, but this decision was not made known to all the societies.

It is admitted by the Government that in the public notice issued by the Registrar in the newspapers, there was no announcement that the Government had decided to allot land based on "first come first served". A large number of societies were therefore not aware of the crucial criterion fixed by the Government. Consequently, many societies had not realized the urgency in sending the applications to the Registrar. Even those societies which had sent their applications on the 20th and 21st of March 1984 were not aware that their claim for allotment was going to be examined based on a first-come, first-served.

The non-disclosure of crucial criterion fixed by the Government for allotment of land, and the jeopardy it caused for several societies, has been conceded by the Government of India before the Court. The Government admitted the norm of "first come, first served" was not disclosed to the public at large, and consequently the societies were not put on notice that land will be allotted on the above-said basis.

Finally, it was decided by the Supreme Court that the Government is duty-bound to refund the amounts paid by the nine cooperative societies towards the cost of land, together with interest. The Government has had the benefit of the amounts deposited by the cooperative societies towards the cost of the land for all these years, and the members of the societies have suffered the loss of interest. The amounts paid by the concerned societies, together with interest at 12% per annum from the date of deposit to the date of a refund, were direct to be paid to end the scam.

Finally, the land was freed by the Supreme Court on 5 April 1989 after four long years, which washed off the second scam of Andrews Ganj but kept it unutilized by the Government for 40 years.

Interestingly, Pavan Sachdeva did not know that after this there will be another scam of Andrews Ganj Land. In fact, he was not aware of any corporation in the name of HUDCO, nor was he involved with any ministry. He was a simple businessman, wanting to make money within the parameters of Government policies. But he always dreamt of owning five-star hotels and big fully automatic industries. He kept developing his business of exports, which was jumping leaps and bounds from 1986 onward.

# Chapter: Twenty-One

*The Ministry of Urban Development Realized that As Per New Master Plan Convention Centre and institutional development can only be done at Andrews Ganj*

After considering all aspects of the matter, the Ministry decided on 4.1.1989, after the approval of the two alternative plans. These would be presented by the Chief Architect to the DUAC with the necessary block models, etc., for the approval to build Government flats for residential accommodation in the General Pool. There was one plan on 27 acres, and another plan on the balance land of 45 acres with green area, etc.

Shri K. Dharmarajan, Joint Secretary, Ministry of Urban Development, sent a DO letter to HUDCO to provide a preliminary possibility analysis which was submitted by HUDCO on assumptions.

The proposal of the Urban Design form at the conceptual stage for the Community Center at Pinjrapole was forwarded by the director of the Ministry of Urban Development to DUAC without the approval of the Land & Development Officer. Initially, the land was 7 acres and was estimated as the cost of land Rs. 28 crores with FAR 100, buildable area 28000 sq. m., construction cost @ Rs. 5000/- per sq. m. Totaling to Rs. 14 crores. It was expected that the sale price would be Rs, 22,000/- per sq. m. as based on a recent sale by NBCC (National Building Construction Corporation). The build space to be given to the Government was 12,700 sq. m. instead of land cost and 5,600 sq. m. to be sold on a no-profit no-loss with an area left on sale for HUDCO, totaling 9,700 sq. m.

For the benefit of the business houses, further amendments to motels, boarding houses, lodging houses, guest houses, hostels, and hotels were given under (building standard) Regulations in 1977 and were modified on 7.6.1989 for permitting guests houses and hotels.

It was proposed on 23 June 1989 by CPWD that layout plan No. TP-32/89 for the Pinjrapole area is already there, but until at the conceptual stage. Due to Afro Asian Games, 1991, there is an urgency to build the proposed four-storied blocks instead of 12 storied or 8 storied blocks.

The ministry under the Minister of Urban Development Smt. Mohsina Kidwai knew very well that the constructions cannot be completed within 21 months of the Afro Asian Games approaching, as it would require testing of electrical and mechanical services for firefighting, lifts, water supply, electric supply, etc. So, the four-storied construction at least in one pocket was recommended as the most desirable to accommodate the requirements of the Afro-Asian Games, which can be completed in 12 to 15 months.

It was known to the Ministry and HUDCO that construction could not be started in less than 6 months, as the scheme is at conceptual approval, and even if this is possible, the clearance of the local body and detailed drawing is made available in 2 months.

Two preliminary estimates covering the construction of 63 type-V flats and 33 type-VI flats were issued in August '88 amounting to Rs. 4.95 crores and Rs. 2.95 crores are already available. These two sanctions can be operated, and the construction of these units taken up if the layout plan is approved by the Ministry, and the approval of DUAC/Local body to the scheme is obtained by the Senior Architect No. TPI/Chief Architect.

The Additional Secretary observed that the Government is interested in the early development of two Community Centers—one near Andrews Ganj. One reason for the urgency is the provision of hotel sites in these community centers. The Additional Secretary suggested the outline of the proposed arrangement, which should be beneficial to both the Government and the agency omitted for development.

It was decided that land will be priced at the predetermined rates prevailing on the date of transfer. The commercial rates will be applicable. The amount of the price of land to the Government will be by way of built-up office accommodation in the community center. It was thought that the proposed arrangement will be beneficial to the Government because it will provide additional office accommodation. It will be of advantage to the development agency because it will generate surpluses that can be utilized for undertaking housing programmers for the poor.

Both the DDA and HUDCO showed interest in the proposition. Simultaneously, neither had any objection if the other body were to take up the work.

In this background, it was decided that HUDCO will undertake the development of a community center at the Andrews Ganj.

HUDCO was to prepare the possibility report, and DDA was to furnish to HUDCO the particulars regarding the provisions in the Master Plan/Zonal Development Plan about various land uses in the Community Center and development controls. CPWD wanted to plan the Community Center with half percent charges, but it was left to HUDCO to decide. It will be decided whether the proposition is viable and if further details regarding the commercial arrangement between the Government and the development agency will be discussed.

CMD HUDCO, Mr. Sharma submitted that prima facie the project appears viable. A proper estimate of returns on investment will be possible only after the urban design studies are completed. HUDCO will be happy to undertake the project on the same terms as offered to the DDA.

The area to be developed as a second convention center and institutional development involve the scheme to be planned in an integrated Urban Design form, like the Habitat Center. Given the above decision, the CPWD proposal to construct the General Pool residential accommodation on this land will have to be given up.

The proposal for the area popularly known as Pinjrapole, located to the South of Andrews Ganj, was examined and the land uses were indicated. Total area 30 Ha (74.1 acres), Residential 13.7 Ha (33.8 acres), Community Centers 7.1 Ha (17.5 acres), Neighbourhood Park 6.0 Ha (14.8 acres), Schools (two Primary + 1 HS) 3.2 Ha (8 acres).

DDA opposed such construction as their work, and not HUDCO's. The proposal for the construction of General Pool Accommodation at Pinjrapole was given up, and the area was to be utilized for the Convention Center and institutional development, but the Ministry until entrusted the work to HUDCO.

# Chapter: Twenty-Two

*Many Eyed Andrews Ganj Land Including Prime Minister's Office*

The Human Resource Development (SAI) also approached the Ministry of Urban Development through their letter dated 26.6.1989 on providing for the construction of 350 flats in Andrews Ganj to accommodate athletes and officials for the Afro Asian Games in November 1991. Sh. R.K. Takkar, Additional Secretary recommended allotting the land out of the land originally allotted to the Nine Societies.

On 4 July 1989, Sh. S.C. Gupta, Director (DC&P), placed the note before the Vice-Chairman that the matter regarding land for Foreign Service Training Institute was discussed with the Vice-Chairman. The estate office suggested in Chanakyapuri is earmarked for District Park, playgrounds, and open spaces. Earlier, there was a proposal to utilize this land for Freight Operation Computer Center for Indian Railways. The matter along with other items was examined in this office, and reference was also made to the Secretary to P.M. vide V.C.'s D.O. letter no. PA/VC/86/222 dated 2.9.1986, along with this D.O. letter, the details of the 4 cases were referred.

The land under reference was also one of the sites for change of land use. In response to this letter vide D.O. letter No. 45/13/86-PMS dated 26.9.1986, Joint Secretary to the Prime Minister, Shri Wajahat Habibullah, informed that the matter was put up to the Prime Minister who has desired that all 4 cases be rejected. However, one of the items about the Indira Gandhi National Open University case was re-submitted for reconsideration. This case was subsequently cleared vide D.O. letter No. 45/193/86-PMS dated 4.2.1987, and the matter was processed, keeping in view the condition of change of land use as stipulated in this letter. The plan indicating the location of the area under reference is enclosed.

Thenceforth, there was inference by the office of the Prime Minister for the Andrews Ganj precious land, and a meeting was held on 5 July 1989 at 11.00 A.M. by the Principal Secretary to the Prime Minister to consider the allotment of a suitable plot for Foreign Service Training Institute. The Ministry of External Affairs was pursuing with the Minister of Urban Development since 30 March 1989 for allotment of land in Andrews Ganj at South Delhi. In the meeting held in the PMO office, along with the secretaries, Urban Development, and Vice Chairman, DDA, it was recommended to the Minister of Urban Development to allot the land.

Again, on 5 July 1989, CPWD on General Pool Housing at Pinjrapole, New Delhi informed the ministry that in the meeting held on 21.12.1988, the alternative layout plans were submitted to the ministry in April 1989 for approval. One was based on 72 acres of land for General Pool Housing, and one was for the balance land considering the pending litigation of 27 acres of land. Now, as the Supreme Court has not upheld the allotment of land to group housing society, the entire land is available for constructing general pool accommodation.

The layout plan No. TP-32/29 prepared based on the utilization of the entire land for general pool housing can therefore be adopted for the construction of general pool accommodation in the Pinjrapole area; subject to the approval of the Ministry regarding break up of several units and approvals of the scheme by DUAC/local body, etc. These two sanctions can be operated, and the construction of these units taken up if the layout plan is approved by the Ministry, and the approval of DUAC/Local body to the scheme is obtained by the Senior Architect No. TPI/Chief Architect. The consolidated proposal of 74 acres is:

The proposal for the area popularly known as Pinjrapole, located to the South of Andrews Ganj, has been examined, which was put up by Shri Chandra Bhallabh, Joint Director, Planning. This area is roughly measuring 30 Ha (74.5 acres) and the land uses have been indicated below:

**Notified Zonal Plan**

- Total area=30 Ha (74.1 acres)
- Residential = 13.7 Ha (33.8 acres)
- Community Centers = 7.1 Ha (17.5 acres)
- Neighbourhood Park = 6.0 Ha (14.8 acres)
- Schools (two Primary + 1 HS) = 3.2 Ha (8 acres)
- Gross density =100 PPA

**As Per Draft PDP 2001**

- Total area = 30.0 Ha (74.1 acres)

- Social and Cultural = 30.0 Ha (74.1 acres)

But Sh. R.K. Takkar, Additional Secretary of the ministry, on 6 July 1989 insisted to Sh. A.C. Panchdhari Addl. Director-General, CPWD, that the accommodation is to be given to the SAI authority for their Afro-Asian Games in 1991. A rough cost estimate of Rs. 105 crores have been sent to Jt. Secretary.

Shri P.S.A. Sundaram stated, “You are requested to give a go-ahead signal for this work at an early date, so as not to lose any time in the matter.” On receipt of the go-ahead signal, approval of the local bodies could be obtained.”

Based on the recommendation of Mr. Takkar, a meeting was proposed to take place on 20 July 1989 at 11:00 A.M. to discuss the scheme of general pool residential accommodation at Pinjrapole, during which the points brought out in this office note No. CE (CZ)/15 (23) 86-W/1952 dated 6 July 1989.

Mr. Takkar had been kept happy by the hoteliers. He insisted during a meeting on 20 July 1989 that the

Government is interested in the early development of two Community centers—one near Andrews Ganj and the other opposite Safdarjung Hospital across the Ring Road. One reason for the urgency is the provision of hotel sites in these community centers. The Additional Secretary suggested the outline of the proposed arrangement, which should be beneficial to both the Government and the agency omitted for development. The land will be priced at the predetermined rates prevailing on the date of transfer. The commercial rates will be applicable.

He proposed that the local bodies, DUAC, DDA, and L&DO will plan and develop the community center according to the guidelines and the regulation on the approvals, as per the Master Plan / Zonal development plan. The proposed arrangement will be beneficial to the Government because it will provide additional office accommodation. It will be of advantage to the development agency because it will generate surpluses that can be utilized for undertaking housing programs for the poor. Both the DDA and HUDCO showed interest in the proposition.

Simultaneously, neither had any objections if the other body were to take up the work. In this background, it was decided that HUDCO will undertake the development of a community center at Andrews Ganj, and the DDA will take up the community center opposite Safdarjung Hospital. Chief Architect, Central P.W.D. requested that the work of planning the community centers should be given to the central P.W. D, for which the charges will be half percent of the estimated cost, which is much cheaper than the rates charged by private architects. It was decided that this decision may be left to the DDA /HUDCO.

It was further agreed that in the event of the Government undertaking the development itself, the theatrics of the chief architect, CPWD, will be appalled. It was agreed that the next meeting will be held on 28 August 1989 at 1600 hours when based on the preliminary feasibility report prepared by HUDCO/DDA, it will be decided whether the proposition is viable. If so, further details regarding the commercial arrangement between the Government and the development agency will be discussed.

# Chapter: Twenty-Three

*Ministry violated General Finance Rules (GFR) Rules282 (3)) and Ignored Instructions of Ministry of Finance*

NBCC (National Buildings Construction Corporation Ltd.), another Public Sector 100% owned by the Ministry of Urban Development, was also keen to get Andrews Ganj land. NBCC had been working as a Project Management Consultant (PMC) for the redevelopment of the Pragati Maidan project of the India Trade Promotion Organization. Several Central Government ministries and various State Governments had been utilizing the services of NBCC as their extended engineering arm.

NBCC's Chairman, Sh. R.C. Kehar wrote a letter dated 25 July 1989 to CMD, HUDCO regarding the development of commercial sites of DDA and Andrews Ganj. HUDCO's CMD, through its letter dated 1.8.1989, suggested that these kinds of projects can be best executed as a joint venture of the consortium and DDA. The cost of land will be treated as a loan from DDA, and the projects could be executed by NBCC on a no-profit, no-loss basis. HUDCO would provide funds for development, and the profits could be shared equally with HUDCO and NBCC.

On 26 July 1989, a meeting was held under the Chairmanship of Sh. R.K. Takkar, along with Additional Secretary with Sh. K. Dharmarajan Joint Secretary, plus HUDCO Chairman, DDA officials, CPWD officials, and Land and Development Officer, Dr. G.S. Jaiya, wherein the interest in hotel sites were shown. It was obvious that Sh. R.K. Takkar and Sh. Dharmarajan was interested in the hotel lobby since they were bribed by some known hoteliers.

It was decided the land would be priced at predetermined rates prevailing on the date of transfer; the Land & Development Officer would participate in its profits. The Community Center will be planned and developed according to the guideline regulations contained in the Master Plan/Zonal development plan.

HUDCO's Chairman had plans behind the scenes to get the Andrews Ganj land, so he met the Private Secretary of Minister for Urban Development and the Minister. After their meeting, the minister spoke to Secretary Shri KC Siva Ramakrishnan, who in turn instructed the additional secretary, Mr. Takkar, to allot the land to HUDCO. Meanwhile, HUDCO was obliging all the officers of the Ministry by sending them vehicles as and when required, not to mention many other gifts to get the land.

A proposal was also sent to the Finance Ministry, which objected to such allotment of Government land to the Public Sector, like HUDCO. He stated no projects involving allotment of Government land/project involving the amount of Rs. 5.00 crores (US Dollar 0.30 crores) should be submitted to the Expenditure Finance Committee, and more than Rs. 20.00 crores (US Dollar 1.23 crores) would require the approval of the cabinet.

The Finance Ministry had further insisted on the amendment of Finance Powers Rules, 1978 explaining that each Ministry may set a Standing Committee on Schemes under the chairmanship of the Secretary with Integrated Financial Advisor, Joint Secretary/Director of the concerned Division as Members, and with provision for inviting representatives of the Planning Commission and any others that the Secretary/Integrated Financial advisor may suggest, for sanction of all such schemes. The

Standing Committee will exercise the delegated powers of the administrative ministries, viz. — sanction of expenditure on schemes already approved by the Ministry of Finance.

It was pointed out that even projects within the competence of the Ministry require prolonged inter-ministerial consultations and approval from the Ministry of Finance and Planning Commission. To avoid this delay, each Ministry/Department should also have an appropriate project implementation committee, as may be deemed necessary for all final proposals.

The Finance Ministry was also informed, as per General Finance Rules (GFR), that the Government land cannot be allotted to a public sector without the approval of the cabinet, and the ministry should refrain from doing so. But the officers favoring HUDCO continued to consider the allotment of Andrews Ganj land to HUDCO, leading to another scam of Andrews Ganj land.

# Chapter: Twenty-Four

*Land Use was Notified in the New Master Plan for Convention Center, Like Vigyan Bhawan*

Sh. M.B. Saxena, Senior Architect, CPWD, through a letter dated 3.8.1989 to Shri J.C. Gambhir, Commissioner Planning, DDA put up an inquiry that there are 71.20 acres called Pinjrapole situated between Andrews Ganj and Sadiq Nagar, also shown in zone F-3 development plan drawing No. L/U-29-A. The detailed site and key plan for the area drawing No. TP-32/28 was enclosed for reference as per the decision of the Ministry of Urban Development vide minutes of the meeting held in the office of additional Secretary on 22.5.1989, and circulated vide No. 17024/B/84/W2 dt. 16.6.89.

The area was set for development by Central Government General Pool Residential Accommodation, comprising type–IV, V, VI, VII, and Hostel accommodation, etc. (i.e., the higher type of Govt. Housing).

It was requested that the development controls for the area be intimated, so a scheme based on those controls could be submitted for the local body's approval. The following should be intimated immediately, so the office can finalize the layout scheme for DUAC's conceptual stage approval:

"Confirmation of the land use of the area, permissible density, permissible ground coverage, permissible F.A.R., height restrictions if any, parking norms w.e.t., multi-storied housing, and any other control," according to the DUAC office. It was proposed to have some accommodation for Afro-Asian Games also in this pocket (to be taken out of General Pool Housing), and the same should be ready to kindly accord this a top priority and furnish the required information at the earliest possible.

Sh. S.K. Sharma, CMD, HUDCO vide letter dated 7.8.1989 to the Shri R.K. Takkar, Additional Secretary, Ministry of Urban Development reminded him to kindly recall our discussion regarding the development of community centers in Delhi.

"You suggested that preliminary economic feasibility may be undertaken. We have investigated the matter. Prima facie the project appears viable. The proper estimate of returns on investment will be possible only after the urban design studies are completed.

HUDCO will be happy to undertake the project on the same terms as are offered to DDA."

The Joint Director of DDA, Zonal Planner, considered the composite zonal plan of zone D 17, 18, 19, and F2 and F3 and to submit along with its report on 10 August 1989.

This matter was discussed by the Vice-Chairman concerning his note on 18 August 1989. A draft letter for sending the same to the Additional Secretary, Ministry of Urban Development was sent.

"On 18 August 1989, Shri K.S. Bains, Vice Chairman, DDA suggested that I did attend this meeting in the chamber of Mr. B.G. Deshmukh. After discussion, it was decided that a suitable plot of land for the institute will be the one in Chanakyapuri near Jesus & Mary College. No further action is, therefore, necessary on our part as regards this institute is concerned. However, as a result of the recent Supreme Court judgment, the allocation of land has become available. We may enter into correspondence with MUD for the transfer of this land to us for its development and disposal. While writing a letter, it would be advisable to include 3 to 4 preliminary proposals as to what could be done here. This could be a Games Village for 1991 Afro Asian Games and a good Conference Hall along with other necessary infrastructure, including even a good hotel where the delegate could stay."

It was submitted on 23 August 1989 that because of the recommendations of the draft PDP-2001, this entire area could be used for a complex similar to the Asian Village Complex, by planning the area comprehensively. A copy of the notified zonal and PDP-2001 land-use plan was placed:

"N. Rajagopalan, Under Secretary to the Government of India, issued the notice for the meeting on 22 August 1989 regarding Development of Community Centers near Andrews Ganj as decided in the meeting held on 26 July 1989 on the above subject. The next meeting to discuss further developments in this matter will be held at 4:00 p.m. on 28tAugust 1989 in the room of Shri R. K, Takkar, Additional Secretary, Ministry of Urban Development, Nirman Bhawan. In pursuance to which Shri K.S. Bains, Vice Chairman,

DDA; Vikas Sadan, Shri K. Dharmarajan, Joint Secretary (LI), Ministry of Urban Development; Shri B. Bhattacharya, Joint Secretary (F), Ministry of Urban /development; Shri S.K. Sharma, CMD, HUDCO; Shri M.K. Rishi, Chief Architect, CPWD; Shri G.S. Jaiya, Land & Development Officer met, and minutes were recorded on 28 August 1989."

The DDA informed that the community center of 7 acres would remain only, and as per Master Plan would be a convention center and balance land institutional. The additional Secretary stated the draft perspective plan will have to be followed unless there are compelling reasons to change any part of the plan. It was observed there is a need for a second convention center in a central locality of Delhi, and the proposed location will be ideal, as it has openings from all four sides and is in a central area.

It was explained by Shri S.C. Gupta that 25% of the area meant for convention centers may be utilized for residential purposes. It was also permissible to build a hotel and, for that matter, hostel accommodation in the Convention Center.

It was decided that the proposed plans be followed; therefore, this would mean that the plans of CPWD to construct General Pool Residential Accommodation on this land would have to be given up. It was decided that a scheme of the overall planning of the entire area may be prepared as an integrated urban design form, like the Habitat Center.

In the given changed position, this area is not available for General Pool Accommodation. The problem of providing accommodation to Afro-Asian Games will have to be discussed. The HUDCO requested to examine the matter and, after consultation with the DDA and others, report within a month whether the construction of hostels attached to the Convention rooms is permissible and will not interfere with the demands of the Afro-Asian Games.

However, the statement continued by saying there is no possibility of expansion of Vigyan Bhavan shortly, though there is a proposal to extend Vigyan Bhavan by adding the area presently occupied by the Vice President's House. This will add an area of about 18 acres to the present Vigyan Bhawan, but this work is not likely to be taken up shortly.

The CPWD would be willing to construct the hostels in the locations which will be marked in the urban design form by HUDCO. Alternatively, a part of the plot could be treated as "residential" in land use to the limited extent of construction accommodation for the Afro-Asian Games, 1991.

The question of which agency should prepare the urban design forms was discussed; however, Vice-Chairman DDA emphasized that planning for all such large areas should be done by DDA. He said DDA had the necessary expertise, and outside help could be requested if needed. After discussion, it was finally decided that urban design for the Andrews Ganj area should be entrusted to HUDCO, while that for West Kidwai Nagar could be entrusted to DDA.

# Chapter: Twenty-Five

*Unauthorized Development of Andrews Ganj at the Behest of The Ministry in the Urgency of 1991 Afro Asian Games*

In a meeting convened by the additional Secretary, Urban Development on 28 August 1989, it was brought to attention that the 30-hectare L&DO site in Andrews Ganj has been zoned in the Master Plan as a part community center and part housing proposed in the revised master plan entirely for an international convention center on an area about 20 acres in size, and the remaining portion will be institutional land. The Additional Secretary remarked that DDA brought this to our notice and wasted eight months discussing the possibility of using Andrews Ganj land as commercial /residential; DDA must be careful in the future.

HUDCO was requested to prepare an urban design for this development. It was then suggested a provision be made in the urban design for guest houses, which can be used for accommodating athletes during the Afro Asian Games in the winter of 1991.

HUDCO enclosed a preliminary report prepared by consultants with HUDCO on the approach to the urban design of the Convention Center. There were two levels of activity complementing each other in the urban design. The first consists of a convention and conference facilities business center, hotel, and multi-level shopping mall in a formal environment. The second was low-rise guest houses and bazaars with eating places, chowks, and streets where traditional and contemporary plastic and performing arts and feats are still performed in an informal setting. The development was to be a unique place for business and cultural interaction, not currently available in Delhi.

In one of the meetings convened by the Additional Secretary (UD), it was expressed that instead of flittering energies on all growth centers, one growth center should be identified for intensive development as a second National Capital instead of the cost of Andrews Ganj land. HUDCO can provide the substantial Central Government office and residential accommodation in the National Capital Region growth center specified by the Central Government, hereby virtually initiating the creation of second national capital. Besides, Rs. 100 crore or so maybe generated as surplus from the development. HUDCO can borrow another RS. 300 to 400 crores for financing infrastructure in NCR and other towns. Thus, the resources generated from land development in Delhi can be effectively utilized for decongesting Delhi itself. This will be a unique yet replicable method of developing new growth centers.

Last year, substantial land was acquired in Meerut with HUDCO's assistance, and another 800 acres is presently under acquisition. A proposal to undertake development in Meerut as joint Ventures of HUDCO and Meerut Development Authority is under consideration. If so desired, the second National Capital can be developed in Meerut.

If the Government decides to promote community centers and housing as per the existing Master Plan, the urban design can be prepared accordingly. In lieu of the cost of land, HUDCO can still provide offices and housing in a growth center, though on a smaller scale. CPWD architects pointed out that DUAC was asking for an integrated urban design. If desired, alternative urban designs can be prepared by HUDCO and CPWD, and the one approved by DUAC can be implemented, or DUAC can request to treat the two as separate projects. It may be mentioned here, as per the Master Plan, the area for the community center is 17 acres and not 7 acres, as earlier intimated by the Ministry. It will need at least six months to prepare the urban design and get DUAC approval.

In the Meeting of 29 August 1989 at HUDCO, it was decided that the site zoned for a community center of 17 acres in the Master Plan for the year 2001 is zoned for an International Convention Center.

The Guesthouses would be low-rise development and two to three stories in modules of 30-40 rooms each. The urban design could be developed considering these guest houses may be low-rise high density, whereas the hotels may be high-rise high density development. This would also facilitate the construction in the shortest period, as the guest houses would be built for the Afro Asian Games scheduled for December 1991.

These guesthouses thereafter would be leased to state Government and private/public sector companies. The lease would be framed in such a way that the guesthouses would be reserved for a fixed number of days to cater for sports events, conventions, etc. In this way, housing facilities would be permanently available for this purpose.

Two hotel sites are proposed to cater for 5 stars and a budget clientele for conventions. The hotel sites would be auctioned for development. The total accommodation available would cover 50% of the capacity of the convention center. A body must be set up to manage the center. This could be a society of members in the hotel and convention trades.

"Mr. Jasbir Sawheny & Associates, Architect through a letter dated 30 August 1989 to Mr. Sharma, CMD HUDCO regarding Andrews Ganj Convention Center in pursuance to our meeting yesterday regarding the above project, enclosed the following documents of brief notes on the meeting the schedule for Urban Design Project, a list of members of the design team, and their bio-data/resume. A feasibility analysis was submitted in which the sale price of hotel land would be Rs 23000/=per Square Meter."

Sh. S.K. Sharma, CMD, HUDCO through a letter dated 31 August 1989 to Sh. K.S. Bains, Vice Chairman, DDA pressed that:

“Kindly refer to our telephonic talk regarding the development of the convention center in Andrews Ganj. We are trying to work out a system whereby the returns from this development will be invested in the development of the growth centers in the National Capital Region, especially in the form of a large Central Government presence to reduce the pressure on Delhi. Such counter investments would be outside the scope of DDA. Moreover, this is a Central Government property, and it is for the Central Government to decide how they would like to develop it.

“As far as observations made by Additional Secretary, MOUD in the meeting held on 28 August 1989 regarding engaging consultants for the urban design study are concerned, we feel that they have merit. Our analysis of the operation of the various public authorities in the country has convinced us that a bulk of creative design work should be commissioned.

“This would introduce various innovative approaches and perceptions and generally lead to appropriate development of the built environment. Architects and planners who chose to join public management should essentially be responsible for design coordination and project management. There appears to be a mistaken notion that an architect is meant only for design when, as in HUDCO, it is also well suited for management positions. Urban designers and architects should play important management and coordination roles in urban authorities.

“Since many disputes with architects are pending and consequently numerous district and community center projects are held up, DDA may, if assigned, find it difficult to execute the Andrews Ganj project within the stringent time limits. I earnestly request you to kindly review the entire matter in the interest of the quality of the built environment. Should you need any assistance from us, we will be happy to provide it.”

Mr. Jasbir Sawheny & Associates, Architect through a letter dated 6 September 1989 to Mr. M.N. Joglekar, Chief Design Development, HUDCO regarding Convention Center, Andrews Ganj:

"This has reference to our meeting of August 30 & 31, 1989, regarding the above project. I am pleased to enclose the following documents requested by you: Brief Note on the project, List of members of the design team and their bio-data, and resume. I have seen the terms and conditions for Urban Design between Noida and M/s. Kuldeep Singh Ram Sharma. In principle, these terms and conditions are in order."

A 33-hectare site in South Delhi had been proposed in the New Master Plan of Delhi for a major convention center. At this site, temporary accommodation is proposed also for sportsmen of the Afro Asian Games in the winter of 1991. The project is briefly described below:

"The site was zoned for a Community Center of 17 acres in the previous master plan, but in the New Master Plan, it is zoned for an International Convention Center."

# Chapter: Twenty-Six

*Finally, Only Convention Center Could Be Developed*

It was also decided on 1 September 1989 that DDA should study the articles of the basic work assigned to HUDCO, and whether such works should be done at Delhi by the DDA or other agencies like HUDCO.

HUDCO held the 39th meeting on 7.9.1989 of the Architectural Advisory Committee, wherein Sh. Jasbir Sawhney, Architect, New Delhi, was appointed as consultant for the proposed Community Center at Andrews Ganj. This meeting was headed by the Executive Director of HUDCO Sh. M.N. Joglekar and the Chairman, Sh. S.K. Sharma.

Sh. S.K. Sharma, CMD, HUDCO, through a letter dated 8 September 1989 to the Shri Siva Ramakrishnan, Secretary, Ministry of Urban Development, reiterated the decision by the Additional Secretary in the meeting held on 28 August 1989.

"In case the Government decides to promote community centers and housing as per the existing Master Plan, the urban design can be prepared accordingly. In lieu of the cost of land, HUDCO can still provide offices and housing in a growth center, though on a smaller scale. CPWD architects pointed out that DUAC was asking for an integrated urban design.

"If desired, alternative urban designs can be prepared by HUDCO and CPWD, and the one approved by DUAC can be implemented, or DUAC can request to treat the two as separate projects. It may be mentioned here that, as per the Master Plan, the area for the community center is 17 acres and not 7 acres, as earlier intimated by the Ministry. It will need at least six months to prepare the urban design and get DUAC approval.

"CPWD officers visited DDA on 18 September 1989, when the file was called to discuss the matter concerning their letter. During the discussion, the officials of CPWD insisted on intimating to them the land use of land in question and permissible development controls, such as ground cover, FAR, etc.

"The gross land use of the site in question, as per the approved zonal plan, is residential with the major portion earmarked for the Community Center and neighborhood part, etc. Whereas in the draft PDP-2001, it is shown for social and cultural under the head of public and semi-public facilities.

"Regarding development controls, it is brought to notice that recently we have forwarded the development control for approval vide file No. F.20 (24) 86-MP about General Pool Housing. After the approval of the development controls, the same would be communicated to the CPWD."

In the meeting on 18 September, 1989 chaired by Sh. R.K. Thakkar, Additional Secretary, Ministry of Urban Development, Government of India, which was attended by VC, DDA, and others from DDA. Sh. S.K. Sharma, Chairman, HUDCO Sh. M.B. Saxena, Chief Architect, CPWD, and others, it was decided that the urban design of Andrews Ganj Area (Pinjrapole area) should be entrusted to HUDCO, while the West Kidwai Nagar could be entrusted to DDA.

The decision was based on the recommendations of the draft perspective plan for the area to be developed as a second convention center and institutional development. The scheme to be planned is an integrated urban design, like the Habitat Center. It was decided, given the decision made by the plans of CPWD to construct General Pool Residential, accommodation on this land will have to be given up.

Mr. M.N. Joglekar, Chief Design Development, HUDCO through a letter dated 18 September 1989 to Mr. Jasbir Sawheny & Associates, Architect confirmed to him:

"Please refer to your letter dated 6.9.1989 concerning the detailed program for project design work of the Convention Center at Andrews Ganj, New Delhi. I am happy to inform you that HUDCO has decided to appoint you as our Consultant for the above-referred project. We are right now in the process of finalizing the Secretary, project brief in consultation with the Ministry and Delhi Development Authority, and I will be signing a formal agreement thereafter.

"The joint director zonal planning of DDA submitted on 19 September 1989 to CPWD regarding the control Government General Pool Residential Accommodation at Pinjrapole, New Delhi. In this regard, it was informed to him that based on the recommendation of the draft PDP-2001, the area to be developed is the second convention center and institutional development. The scheme to be planned is an integrated urban design form, like the Habitat Center.

"Delhi Development Authority (Zonal Plan Section), Convention Center at Siri Fort the draft Master Plan for Delhi 2001—has recommended the setting up of a convention center of international standards with all modern facilities on Khel Gaon Marg near Asia Village. An area of about 30 hectares has been earmarked as public & semi-public use for socio-cultural facilities. Adjacent to this, about four hectares of the area have been earmarked for a modern shopping center on similar lines as those of departmental stores in various developed countries."

The convention center would have the following major components to be planned in an integrated manner:

"Main convention center complex, Five-Star hotel with a capacity of about six hundred rooms, out of which 50% of the accommodation would cater to the net-se affluent clients. Medium capacity guest houses ranging from 20 to 30 rooms, providing total accommodation of about 1000 rooms.

“A very modern shopping center which would cater to international tourists/visitors and affluent society of Delhi and other areas. A fully equipped training institute, which would impart training to personnel, that is to man various facilities required for the conduct of conventions/conferences of international levels.

“These would range from secretarial training to translators to interpreters to media/communication facilities of a high standard.” An administrative office complex which would house the office of the agencies/society would be designated to monitor and regulate the development of the project and would be responsible for the conduct of convention/conference, etc., and continued maintenance and upkeep.”

# Chapter: Twenty-Seven

*HUDCO Was Favored as against CPWD and DDA To Go Ahead Contrary to Land Use*

On 19 September 1989, Shri Anil Barai, Deputy Director, CPWD stated, “Please refer PU at -1/C from Senior Architect, CPWD regarding the Central Government General Pool Residential accommodation at Pinjrapole, New Delhi. In this regard, please refer note of Joint Director (P)-I on page 3-4/N. As per the decision based on the recommendation of the draft PDP-2001, the area to be developed as a second convention center and institutional development, the scheme to be planned is an integrated Urban Design form like the Habitat Center.

“Because of the above decision, the CPWD proposal to construct the General Pool Residential accommodation on this land will have to be given up. If agreed, we may inform the Senior Architect, CPWD.”

My dear readers, here it is very clear as per allocation of works and buildings, as well as land developments, it was either CPWD or DDA could only develop Andrews Ganj, but still, the Congress Government minister of the Ministry of Urban Development had instructed that work should be given to HUDCO for the best internal reasons known to the Government or the officers concerned at the relevant time. Not only this land could be developed only for the construction of the Convention Centre for Government, but still was advised to go ahead with other uses that were contrary to the land use.

Sh. S.C. Gupta, Director (DC&P)[5] on 19 September 1989 admitted that no reply is required for the letter under reference, as the Government has decided the site is to be used mainly for a Convention Center and not for the Central Government Staff Housing Site and will be earmarked for a Convention Center in PDP-2001 (modified). Another file No. F/1881 on the subject is also placed below, wherein there is a reference from Commissioner (Planning) 1989, that will be examined.

Sh. S.K. Sharma, CMD, HUDCO through Office Memorandum dated 27 September 1989 to Sh. Jasbir Sawhney, Architect regarding Andrews' Ganj Urban

[5] (Government of SKIKKIM)

Design. The following may be incorporated in the informal zone being created in the urban design:

"A cluster of studios for artists and craftsmen; Eastern and Western, Akhadas of Gymnasiums. Billiard saloon and stalls for games of skill. In the landscape, small stools with chess, ludo, snakes & ladder boards, etc. etched on them, may be made. Informal stages for open-air, street, and terrace theater. Suitable informal niches partly covered, partly open for cold drinks, chat shops, etc., should be properly designed.

"The economic viability of the above facilities may be seen. A sizable cluster of Laurie Baker homes, guest houses, and bazaar will be made in the urban design.

"The urban designer may visit some of the existing community centers, see the shortcoming in the facilities, and incorporate appropriate elements in the design. Wherever possible, open spaces may be used for such informal activities to reduce costs.

"The timeline was fixed for completion of guesthouses by 31 October 1991, and would be operational by November 1991."

Sh. S.K. Sharma, CMD, HUDCO through a letter dated 4 October 1989 to Sh. K Dharmarajan, Joint Secretary, MOUD:

"Based on the discussion we had the other day, our architects have prepared a revised program for the development of the Andrews Ganj area, consisting of a Community Center with convention facilities, guest houses, Government transit accommodation, and Government housing. We also discussed and generally approved the market survey proposed submitted by the Indian Market Research Bureau since you were not able to attend the meeting. I will appreciate it if you would go through these documents and communicate concurrence to the program, so that we may go ahead with the market survey.

"One difficult question is the size of the convention hall. Large halls are generally underutilized. They are needed mainly for inaugural sessions of conventions.

Business sessions rarely have more than 500 participants. If we look conjunctively at Siri Fort Auditorium of 3000 capacity, the inaugural function can be in Siri Fort (which is mostly vacant during daytime) and business sessions in the proposed Convention Center. If this is acceptable, then the convention center would not have a hall of a capacity exceeding 800 to 1000, which can be divided into two rooms of capacity 400 to 500. This needs serious thought."

On 11 October 1989, it was confirmed that referring to 26 July 1989 minutes, it was decided that HUDCO had been assigned to develop a community center, including a convention center, and no formal administrative approval is required. Truly speaking, such an assignment could have not been given to HUDCO that also without formal administrative approvals, but CPWD and DDA officials kept their mouths shut, being afraid of being shunned by the concerned Minister. The officials were a puppet in the hands of the Government.

HUDCO started on 13 October 1989, the Ministry had proposed to entrust the urban design of the Andrews Ganj area to HUDCO. Some guesthouses and houses are to be ready by the winter of 1991 for the Afro Asian Games. JS (L&I) informed that the file has been submitted to the Urban Development Minister for approval, which is getting delayed on account of preoccupation with Parliament and other pressing business.

"Our Architects have submitted a proposal for land and soil survey and market survey. They have stressed that unless the surveys are commissioned by the 15th of this month, it will not be possible to maintain the Afro Asian Games deadline. Since these surveys will inevitably have to be done for any type of urban design study, and since the costs involved are small in comparison to the total size of the project, these studies may be immediately commissioned pending formal approval of the Government."

Sh. Harcharanjit Singh, Dy. Secretary, Ministry of Urban Development, through a letter dated

16.10.1989 to Shri S. K. Sharma, CMD, HUDCO as follows:

"The Ministry has been considering the utilization of 74 acres of land in Pinjrapole Area. Secretary, during a discussion with Addl. D.G., CPWD, on 27.9.1989, had desired that CPWD should come up with revised plans for utilization of the land earmarked for residential use in the existing zonal plan. He has now desired to discuss the plan for the construction of General Pool accommodation on 17.10.1989 at 12:30 p.m. along with the proposals for the development of a Community Center in the area. I would, therefore, request you to kindly attend the meeting along with the necessary details of the proposals for utilization of the land available in the Pinjrapole Area."

Sh. S.K. Sharma, CMD, HUDCO through Office Memorandum dated 18 October 1989 to the Secretary, Chief Architect–CPWD and Sh. Jasbir Sawhney, Urban Development Consultant regarding Andrews Ganj Urban Design:

"In a meeting convened by Secretary, MOUD, on the 17 October 1989, it was decided that because of the urgency to complete the construction of housing units required for the Afro Asian Games in the winter of 1991, these units may be located near the road leading to MoolChand Hospital and taken up for construction by CPWD after obtaining DUAC approval. Detailed urban design study for the entire area can follow.

"It was further decided that HUDCO would undertake an integrated urban design study for the community center and housing, on the understanding that suitable arrangements will be entered into between the Ministry and HUDCO for the development of the area after the design is finalized."

Interestingly, the decision was after the approval of DUAC, but until 1999, no final approval of revised layout plans was done, as everything was implemented based on the conceptual approval. The Government and the officers concerned let HUDCO build the buildings without the approval of any other statutory bodies, leading to total violations. But my dear reader's Violations by Government authorities are not called violations in India, and they do not need to be ratified unless they are brought to the knowledge of courts.

Chief Architect, CPWD agreed to make available the plans of the units proposed for the Afro Asian Games to HUDCO Urban Design consultants, so that they may locate them appropriately in keeping with the proposed overall urban design. Because of the above decision, it was decided on 26 October 1989 that the CPWD proposal to construct the General Pool residential accommodation on this land will have to be given up.

The CPWD was dropped point-blank when CPWD and DDA were willing to develop and construct after approvals at the cost of a half percent. HUDCO was agreed by the Government to give one and a half percent without any substance or reason. But so, this is the Government, they are God, and they can do anything they like without any justification, as they have power.

# Chapter: Twenty-Eight

*DDA Asked Ministry to Transfer the Land to Them*

In the meantime, the new master plan was prepared by DDA and notified in August 1990, in which the Andrews Ganj land was reserved for a convention center, like the Vigyan Bhawan kinds. Thus, the General Pool Accommodation plan was to be abolished.

Vigyan Bhawan is a premier convention center of the Government of India in New Delhi. Built in 1956, over the years it has been the venue for conferences of national and international stature, seminars, and award ceremonies attended by distinguished world leaders and dignitaries, including Commonwealth Heads of Government Meeting (CHOGM) in 1983, 7th Summit of the Non-Aligned Movement (NAM), March 7-12, 1983, and SAARC Summit. It is managed by the Directorate of Estates under the Ministry of Urban Development, Government of India, and maintained by CPWD.

As per the new master plan of Delhi, it was notified that a major convention center in Andrews Ganj was planned by DDA, along with the temporary accommodation for the Afro Asian Games coming in the winter of 1991. The Convention Center planned to have accommodations for 5000 persons, a hotel, economic hotel, guest houses, shopping centers, restaurants, medical facilities, an institution for the training personnel, communication media and conventions, and offices of the Management Society. Plus, infrastructure buildings including an electrical substation, fire station, post office, etc., parking for cars and buses, parks, and green areas.

Shri K.S. Bains, Vice Chairman, DDA through his letter dated to Shri R.K. Takkar, Additional Secretary, MOUD asked for Andrews Ganj land:

"A large chunk of land measuring about 30 hectares in Pinjrapole located in the south of Andrews Ganj is a major part of which was earlier allotted by the Ministry of Urban Development to various Group Housing Cooperative Societies has become available; As a result of a recent Supreme Court judgment where allocation has been struck down. In PDP-2001 (modified) and submitted to the Government for approval, this land is proposed to be utilized for a project like the Asian Village complex, based on a comprehensive scheme.

"This land could be used as Games Village 1991 (Afro-Asian Games)[6], a good Conference Hall, along with other necessary infrastructure, including even a good hotel where the delegates could stay."

He, therefore, suggested that this land may please be transferred to the DDA for such a comprehensive scheme on the lines indicated above.

"On 18 October, reference to the meeting with the secretary given by HUDCO that because of the urgency of the Afro Asian Games in winter 1991, HUDCO should go ahead. It was further decided that HUDCO would undertake integrated urban design for the community center and housing, on the understanding that suitable arrangements will be entered into between the ministry and HUDCO after a design is finalized."

---

[6] (Inside the Games)

But still, Sh. M.B. Saxena, Senior Architect, CPWD, through a letter dated 2.11.1989 to the Shri S.K. Sharma, CMD, HUDCO as follows:

"Please refer to your above-quoted letter addressed to CPWD regarding the Residential Scheme of General Pool Government at Pinjrapole, New Delhi."

The minutes of the meeting held in the office of the Secretary of Urban Development on 17 October 1989 are still awaited; however, CPWD never committed or agreed that HUDCO shall do the urban form or layout of the entire residential area. Only the urban form of a community center with a plot area of 17.6 acres was to be developed by HUDCO, and that is a community center for the entire zone F.3.

It may be added here that the Residential Scheme prepared by CPWD, which has also been discussed above, said in the meeting was never rejected by the Secretary. He only suggested some change in the location of one type-IV four-storied quarters for S.A. of India, so that it could proceed for local body approval immediately without the wait of an urban

form for a community center which HUDCO Architect required in 3.5 months.

"The revised scheme is almost ready in this office and shall be presented to the Secretary Urban Development Ministry for his approval before submitting it to the local body."

Sh. S.K. Sharma, CMD, HUDCO through a letter dated 1 November 1989 to Sh. K. C Sivaramakrishan, Secretary, Ministry of Urban Development:

"In the meeting convened by you on 17 October 1989 regarding Andrews' Ganj Urban Design, it was agreed that because of the urgency, the flats required for Afro Asian Games will be constructed as per CPWD type design. The location and layout of these flats would be indicated by HUDCO to fit in the overall integrated urban design. This is important since the road circulation and landscape will need to be properly harmonized.

"Another month is being lost in decision-making, and the short time available is being further squeezed. The final and firm direction of the Ministry may kindly be communicated urgently so that preparation of the urban design may be taken up."

In the said meeting held on 3 November 1989, it was finally decided the urban design for the Andrews Ganj area should be entrusted to HUDCO. The Joint Director (Planning), vide his note on page 3 and 4/N. also gave earlier these observations It was noted that now no action appears to have been pending on DDA's part, as the work has been entrusted to HUDCO.

Ongoing through the minutes placed on 3 November 1989, it was observed that the proposal for the construction of General Pool Accommodation at Pinjrapole has been given up, and instead this area is to be utilized for the convention center and institutional development following the proposed provisions in the draft PDP-2001 (modified).

Now after the land use of Andrews Ganj land as per the Master Plan changed to Convention Center, HUDCO was eyeing the Andrews Ganj land and proposed to develop the Convention Center on the 17 acres. It would generate income by building guest houses of 40 rooms, each with three stories. The guest houses would be built for the Afro Asian Games scheduled for December 1991. These guesthouses thereafter would be leased to state Government and private/public sector companies. The total accommodation available in the hotel and guesthouses would cover 50% of the capacity in the convention center.

The plan included two types of shopping centers; one in the form of an enclosed, multi-level shopping mall. This would be provided adjacent to the convention center and the hotels. Public restaurants would be provided in both the formal and informal sectors, catering to their needs. The guesthouses would use these restaurants for their customers, and the shopping mall would have restaurants at that end. The restaurants of both formal and informal sectors would be a central part of a polyclinic, and the first-aid post will be provided in the center for the use of the visitors and residents.

The land for the convention center is a major resource. HUDCO proposes to develop the convention center out of this resource and generate an additional fund. To this fund, HUDCO proposes to add Rs. 100 crores for investment in a growth center of the national capital region. This initial investment would attract an additional Rs. 500-600 crores from financial institutions, whereby an alternative center to Delhi can be developed in the National Capital Region. They had the potential to exploit the strong principle of resources developed in Delhi, used for alternative towns in the NCR.

# Chapter: Twenty-Nine

*Congress Government and Officers Hand in Glove*

CPWD eyeing the Andrews Ganj land submitted through Sh. M.K. Rishi, Addl. Chief Architect CPWD through a letter dated 8.11.1989 to the Shri R.K. Takkar, Addl. Secretary, Ministry of Urban Development regarding General Pool Housing at Pinjrapole (Andrews Ganj):

"You would kindly recall we had a discussion on this project on the revised design prepared by Shri M.B. Saxena, Senior Architect (H & TP). After this meeting, this case was deliberated within CPWD and we have concluded that we are interested in preparing the total integrated design including the commercial area contained in the Community Center. I hope the Ministry of Urban Development will consider this request. It is requested that the finalized requirements of the Community Center on the 17.6-acre plot be made available to help us in preparation for the integrated design. As desired, this office is required to get approval from the Municipal Bodies to out scheme for taking up the construction of residential areas required for Afro-Asian games. A meeting is requested with the Secretary, Ministry of Urban Development, to be kindly arranged before we approach the Municipal Bodies for obtaining an approval on the scheme."

CPWD reiterated through Sh. M.K. Rishi, Addl. Chief Architect, CPWD through a letter dated 9.11.1989 to the Shri Harish Chandra, DG (Works) regarding General Pool Housing at Pinjrapole (Andrews Ganj):

"The revised design was prepared consequent upon the decision taken in a meeting with the Secretary, Ministry of Urban Development and discussed with Addl. Secretary, Ministry of Urban Development and further discussed with Addl. Secretary, Ministry of Urban Development on 7.11.1989. He was requested to arrange for a meeting with the Secretary, Urban Development so that the same could be shown to him before processing the case further.

"During the meeting, Secretary, Urban Development decided that we should present the case to DUAC for obtaining approval to the General Pool Housing on housing for Afro-Asian Games. He had apprehension over DUAC requiring a total urban design for the complete site, including the Community Center. He believed that the design of the Community Center would be given to HUDCO.

"He had further given the option that both HUDCO and CPWD should prepare a comprehensive development plan. Out of the two designs prepared, the Ministry of Urban Development would process the design in which they find more suitable. The undersigned stated that the total project including the Community Center should be entrusted to CPWD."

The case was discussed with DG (Works) in the presence of SA (H&TP) I, SA (H&TP) who believed that CPWD should undertake this challenge. The matter was further deliberated on 8.11.989 in the room of the Chief Architect, where again SA (H&TP) was emphatic about his earlier remarks. Therefore, in consultation with him, the attached note has been sent to the Secretary Ministry of Urban Development. This is placed for the information of DG (Works).

On 10 November 1989, HUDCO, CMD wrote to the ministry that the above matter was discussed in a meeting in the Ministry on 17.10.1989. The meeting was chaired by Secretary, Urban Development and was attended by CMD, HUDCO, JS (Land), HUDCO's Architect Consultant, Senior Architects of CPWD, and CF®, HUDCO. The minutes have yet to be received.

"I have been regularly contacting Shri Charcharanjeet Singh," said Deputy Secretary (Lands) in this connection.

"He informed that the file has been submitted to UDM for approval of the proposal. I also spoke to Shri Dharmarajan, JS (Land) in this connection on 8.11.1989. He also stated that as soon as a final decision is taken, HUDCO will be informed."

During the meeting on 17.10.1989, it was agreed that the flats required for Afro Asian Games will be constructed as per CPWD design. The location and layout of these flats would be decided by HUDCO's Consultant who would also do the urban design work for the entire area available for the project.

It was pointed out by CMD, HUDCO that as the work relating to preparing an urban design for the entire area would involve substantial expenditure, the same should be reimbursed to HUDCO by the Ministry in case it was subsequently decided that the various items of work will be executed by some other agencies. Though the Secretary of Urban Development was seemingly inclined to agree with the logic, no clear decision was stated in this regard. CMD, HUDCO had also written to Secretary Urban development on 1.11.1989 regarding this point.

Since CPWD wanted to take the Andrews Ganj land instead of HUDCO, Sh. M.B. Saxena, Senior Architect, CPWD through a letter dated 15.11.1989 to the Shri Jaswir Sawhney, Architect regarding General Pool Government Housing at Pinjrapole, New Delhi:

"Please find here enclosed all the necessary information as following about the meeting held in the office of Sh. R.K. Takkar, Addl. Secretary, Ministry of Urban Development: Plinth area norms and framed by Government of India, Ministry of Urban Development vide No. 17020/2/86 dt. 25.8.87photocopy 5 pages. Survey site plan for the entire site of Pinjrapole Drawing No. 3228TP. Layout Plan showing the scheme discussed in Secretary,

Ministry of Urban Development, 8 room on 17.10.89Drawing No. TP-34261 (This scheme is now being changed but can, however, only be referenced for your urban form of the Community Center being undertaken by HUDCO)."

# Chapter: Thirty

*R.K. Takkar, Additional Secretary Interests*

Sh. R.K. Takkar, Ministry of Urban Development who had instructions from the top to give Andrews Ganj land to HUDCO, due to a letter dated 20.11.1989 to the Shri M.K. Rishi, Chief Architect, CPWD making fool of CPWD to keep the files rightly wrote:

"Kindly refer to correspondence resting with your D.O. No. SA (H&TP) I/188 dated 8.11.1989, regarding General Pool Housing at Pinjrapole. In the meeting taken by me on 7 November 1989, you and your colleague had mentioned that you would not be interested in taking up the urban design of the whole area, including the Community Center. Now I am glad to note that you have reconsidered your position and should be interested in the total design.

Please go ahead and do the needful.

"For requirements of the Community Center, you may consult the Master Plan, 1962 of the draft PDP, 2001. Wherever necessary, you may consult the concerned officers of the DDA. Simultaneously, HUDCO will also be preparing a total Urban Design for the area. They may be given necessary assistance by the Central PWD as and when required. In the meantime, as discussed, the conceptual plans for the residential portion may be submitted to the Delhi Urban Art Commission through the concerned local body very urgently."

An empowered committee for Andrews Ganj land was made by HUDCO and the meeting was held on 1 December 1989 in the chamber of HUDCO's Chairman wherein Shri SK Sharma, CMD, Shri Mulkh Raj, Director Finance attended along with Shri Joglekar, Executive Director, Shri Jasbir Sawhney, Consultant Architect, and Shri B Bahl, Chief Finance Project of HUDCO's officers:

As per the letter of the Addl. Secretary MOUD dated 7 November 1989, an integrated urban design of the Community Center, Housing and Master Plan Green are to be prepared. However, Shri MB Saxena, Senior Architect, CPWD informed on the phone that because of the urgency of flats needed for the Afro Asian Games, they have already prepared a layout of the housing and submitted it to the MCD for onward submission to DUAC.

Shri Jasbir Sawhney, Architect said there were various complex issues specifically for transportation and the impact of the proposed flyover on Tito Road, which needed to be resolved before preparing the urban design. The integration and landscaping of the Master Plan Green also needed to be worked out.

After discussion, it was agreed that HUDCO would commission the architects for the Community Center urban design, and while preparing this urban design, the architects would do preliminary level work on the overall circulation and blocking of the housing and Master Plan Green. If the approach was approved by the authorities, they can then be commissioned for the urban design of the housing. It was decided that for the Community Center, architects would do the detailed urban design of all facilities excluding hotels; they would do only concept-level urban design.

It was thus decided that at present the agreement with the consultant may be signed for a detailed urban design for the Convention Center, shopping center and restaurants, administration & service center, guest houses and site development works. As far as the hotel's component, the concept stage urban design will consist of an overall layout plan; indicating the land use, different components circulation patterns and basic site development concepts (landscaping), and overall blocking of the various buildings. Besides the above, detailed urban design will include the elevational control drawings, and other regulations if required, including detailed dispositions of various uses in a building and landscaping details.

It was also decided that after completion of this urban design exercise and its submission to the concerned authorities, the further scope of work will be decided.

It was further agreed by HUDCO to award the work of site survey and soil investigation for the reduced scope of work covering the Community Center area only and overall boundary of the entire site to the lowest tenderer, viz, M/d. Geotech Consultants Private Ltd. as recommended by the Consultant. As the scope of work has been reduced, the Consultant will provide a revised schedule of the work involved based on which the work would be awarded.

It was decided to award the work of market survey to M/s. IMRB at a total cost of Rs. 1.10 lacs with the following payment schedule:

"The consultant explained in detail the need for getting the Traffic Survey conducted. It was decided to award the work of the Traffic Survey to M/s. Satish Jeevan & Associates at a total cost of Rs. 17,500/-.

"The next meeting of the Empowered Building Committee was to be held on 18.12.1989 at noon. It was decided to invite Chief Architect, CPWD, Additional Secretary, MUD, and Mr. Dharmarajan, Joint Secretary (LI), MUD in the next meeting, as the Consultant will present preliminary design in the next meeting."

It is interesting that without any formal decision, HUDCO went on before all the planning and construction were started without the Ministry of Finance in the loop.

# Chapter: Thirty-One

*Government Under V.P. Singh*

Vishwanath Pratap Singh is also known as V. P. Singh was an Indian politician who was the 8th Prime Minister of India from 2.12.1989 to 10.11.1990. In the 1989 elections, the National Front, with the support of the BJP, formed the government and Singh became the 8th Prime Minister of India from 2.12.1989 and 6.12.1989. Sh. Murasoli Maran was made Minister of Urban Development and remained until 10.11.1990. The Government was a coalition Government from DMK Party; Tamil Nadu wanted to make money in the period he became the minister.

HUDCO held the second meeting on 22 December 1989 of the empowered committee for the Andrews Ganj project. An area of 27 hectares in CMD chamber in which the same officers and the Architect, Jasbir Sawhney, was Urban Design consultant for HUDCO. In the meeting K Dharmarajan, Joint Secretary (Land) MOUD, MK Rishi, Chief Architect, and MB Saxena, Senior Architect, CPWD, and HC Gupta, Director (Planning) DDA were also present. The discussions which took place on the presentation were minute separately:

"The chief architect, CPWD observed that as the CPWD survey is not based on the triangulation system, proper angles of the site were not available in their survey report. He, therefore, requested that the site survey may be conducted by DUDCO for the entire area of over 71 acres of land available at Andrews Ganj, but the soil investigation can be done by HUDCO for the community center alone. The suggestion was agreed to by the committee.

"CF (R) mentioned that the soil investigation agency, M/S Geotech Consultants Pvt Ltd, has requested the association of a full-time authorized representative of HUDCO for all the time to be present for the fieldwork. EDD opined that this was generally not the practice but would be in the interest of the client. It was decided that the urban design consultants will liaise with the soil investigation agency to ensure that it is completed to their satisfaction. The consultant's mat associates with the soil investigation agency as and when required."

The proposal to appoint M/s KK Soni & Co for certifying the payments and attending to the items of work relating to this project on a consolidated fee of Rs2000 per month was approved.

The meeting was also held by Sh. K.K. Takkar, Additional Secretary on 22 December 1989 along with the same members and the minutes were recorded:

"Shri Jasbir Sawhney, Urban Design Consultant, HUDCO presented a preliminary urban design proposal for the government land in Andrews Ganj. Shri Sawhney gave an account of the location and its environs, the road linkages, and the traffic problems. He informed that to properly regulate the traffic on the Tito Marg, the city authorities were planning a fly-over at the intersection which will have to be taken into consideration while designing the circulation. He observed that the three large office complexes, namely Bhikaji Cama Place, Lodhi Institutional Area, and Nehru Place had already come upon the east, north, and southwest of the site and a fourth one was contemplated on the south, and as such there should be less component of office and more of community facilities in the urban design."

In illustrating a basic approach, the consultants said they were proposing two multistorey hotels, a convention center, and a shopping mall around the semi-circular podium, and parking would be provided below. The plan allocated a large public plaza, effectively taking care of parking needs. While this would constitute the formal activity in the urban design, an interesting component would be a low-rise guest house complex with streets and courts where various activities that would enrich civic life could be planned.

Shri Gupta, Director Planning, DDA said facilities like libraries, post offices, etc. should be incorporated in the community center. Shri Takkar, Addl. Secretary MOUD observed it would not be appropriate to a large convention center, but conference facilities attached to the hotel or guest house complex can be provided. The urban design approach was appreciated, and the consultant was requested to detail out the proposal.

Insofar as Master Plan Green of 18 acres is concerned, the consultants expressed this would be most desirable to consolidate it between the community center and housing instead of fragmenting it into patches about the housing. Various public facilities like open-air theater, etc. linked with the Community Center as well as housing will be designed in the Master Plan Green.

As far as the housing is concerned, the consultant indicated that circulation keeping in view the proposed fly-over had been worked out and CPWD could detail out the housing unit.

Shri Takkar Addl. Secretary strongly felt that this would not be a correct approach; an integrated urban design in which the height, form, and texture of the housing had a relationship with the community center should be developed. He said CPWD can work out an alternative inter-graded scheme. After discussing, it was felt that HUDCO should develop an integrated urban design for the Community Center Master Plan Green and housing, then present it to the Government within a fortnight or so keeping in view the urgency of providing accommodation for the afro Asian games in the winter of 1991.

CMD, HUDCO felt that a monitoring committee for implantations of the urban design would be necessary. Director finance, HUDCO observed that HUDCO would have to invest a substantial amount in preparation of the urban design and wanted to know how this would be reimbursed. Addl. Secretary and JS (lands) said implantation of the urban design for the Community Center would be entrusted to HUDCO. A suitable arrangement would be worked out, which will fully take care of the investment made by HUDCO in the preparation of the urban design.

# Chapter: Thirty-Two

*Ministry Involved in Illegal Constructions*

On 22 December 1989, HUDCO submitted the Project being the Urban Design for Community Center, Andrews Ganj, New Delhi submitting the report—Preliminary Evaluation Stage:

"Introduction of the site of 71.2 acres at Andrews Ganj (Pinjrapole)[7] is shown in the zonal development plan of the Delhi Master Plan for the development of group housing, a zonal park, and a Community Center. In order to take up the urban design of the Community Center, it was necessary to carry out an analysis of the site and its immediate surrounding to create the necessary linages to the network of roads and open spaces in the region which would therein influence the location and shape of facilities with the site."

- **Land Use:** As per the Zonal Development Plan, the broad land use for the site is as follows:
- **Community Center:** 17.6 acres, Zonal Green–18.0 acres, Housing35.6 acres Total 71.2 acres. In principle, the site is divided into

[7] (Details of Land Allotments)

two parts, with Housing on the east side towards Tito Marg and Community Center, with the Zonal Green on the West Side towards Khelgaon Road.

- **Community Center:** The Community Center is proposed on 71 hectares or 17.6 acres along Khelgaon road to the zonal park acting as a buffer between Community Center and is proposed with the following facilities.
- **Conference Center, Hotel:** 5 Star & Economy, Shopping Center, and Restaurants, Administration/Service Center and Guest Houses.

The minutes of the meeting chaired by Secretary, Urban Development relating to the Andrews Ganj project held on 28 December 1989 were recorded in the presence of Shri KC Sivaramakrishnan, Secretary (UD), Shri K. Dharmarajan, Joint Secretary (LI), Shri Sk Sharma, CMD, HUDCO, and Shri Jasbir Sawney, Architect Consultant that:

"The urban design concept was explained by the consultant to the Secretary (UD). CMD, HUDCO said that in the meeting held on 22 December 1989 chaired by Additional Secretary, MOUD, it was desired that HUDCO should develop an integrated urban design for the community center and housing. He enquired whether HUDCO should get involved in preparing the urban design of housing. After discussion, it was decided that, based on the site analysis done by HUDCO consultants, CPWD would design the housing."

Sh. B. Bahl through a letter dated 29 December 1989 M/s. K.K. Soni & Co. Chartered Accountants that HUDCO had been assigned the work of preparing the concept of urban design and for the community center project at Andrews Ganj, New Delhi. M/s. Jasbir Sawhney & Associates have been appointed as HUDCO's Architect Consultant for preparing the concept of urban design. Plus, conducting site survey and subsoil investigation, market survey, and traffic survey, etc. The works have also been awarded to various professional firms.

In their minutes, "Your work will commence with effect from 1.1.1990. You will place the services of one of your officials at the disposal of HUDCO for handling all the work relating to this project. We shall be grateful if you kindly convey your acceptance of the above assignment and the terms and conditions mentioned above and also arrange to place one of your officials on this work with effect from 1.1.1990."

Entire meetings with the Additional Secretary were known to the secretary but to circumvent HUDCO's Chairman, Sh. S.K. Sharma through a letter dated 1.1.1990 to Shri KC Sivaramakrishnan, Secretary, Ministry of Urban Development, Nirman Bhawan insisted for the Andrews Ganj Land:

"Kindly recall our discussion on 28 December 1989 regarding the urban design of community center and housing in Andrews Ganj. He enclosed a copy of the report containing a site analysis prepared by HUDCO's which analyzed the traffic and circulation issues and delineates the area for housing to enable CPWD to plan the housing.

"The conceptual urban design of the Community Center and Master Plan Green being prepared by

HUDCO will be ready by 15 January 1990 for submission to the authorities. A Joint Secretary (Lands) may be designated as the officer-in-charge for coordinating the urban design being prepared by HUDCO and CPWD for submission to MCD and piloting through DUAC."

HUDCO recorded that in the meantime, the minutes of the meetings held on 22.12.1989 under the chairmanship of Additional Secretary, MOUD, and 28.12.1989 under the Chairmanship of Secretary, MOUD has since been received from the Ministry. It has been mentioned in the minutes of the meeting held on 22.12.1989, that the Additional Secretary and Joint Secretary (Lands) stated implementation of the urban design for the Community Center would be entrusted to HUDCO and that suitable arrangement would be worked out which will fully take care of the investments made by HUDCO in preparation of the urban design.

# Chapter: Thirty-Three

*HUDCO place -Andrews Ganj Land Valuing Rs.5000 Crores Wasted*

Secretary Shri KC Sivaramakrishnan, Ministry of Urban Development, and the Minister did not bother with the current land use of Andrews Ganj for the Convention which was bi passed. The concern of land use was also bi passed and the instructions of the Ministry of Finance were also bi passed.

The possession of the land was given to HUDCO without any documents or any sanctions. HUDCO started the constructions at Andrews Ganj in confidence with the Ministry of Urban Development, Land & Development Office. The entire scheme is illegal and resulted in a scam. HUDCO had taken steps towards construction without any approvals from any of the local bodies. The land use was not residential or a Community Center or a convention center as had been notified by the current Master Plan.

But ministries under Congress Governments or hanging Governments were Rajas means king of their kingdom and could do anything they felt like. It is seen here the Additional Secretary was all in the urban design of such a precious, huge land and he was acting like he was the owner of this land. Delhi Urban Art Commission was reluctant to approve the layout, and they even kept rejecting it. No building plans were submitted to Municipal Corporation, nor were they approved by the fire department, nor by the Land and Development office, or Delhi Development Authority.

There was a press clipping of Nav Bharat Times in August 1991 that the unauthorized construction is being carried out by HUDCO in the Pinjrapole area. But still, the entire construction was carried out unauthorized, which was in the knowledge of the then Secretary, Joint Secretary, L&DO. The Minister of the monitoring committee consisted of all these offices, but let HUDCO construct unauthorized constructions at Andrews Ganj, and without any allotment of the subject land in their favor.

All the doings by the Congress Government regarding Andrews Ganj land after the independence of India, in between hanging Governments, and again Congress Government from 1991 to 1996 under Prime

Minister, Sh. P.V. Narsimha Rao could not be ratified by any next Government.

All the scams, whether disclosed by the media or not, were under the previous Governments in power. A study by a Berlin-based NGO has pegged India as the most corrupt nation in the Asia-Pacific region without considering the other hidden scams. The eight scams exposed show why we have a poor rating while many of the scams like Rs. 5000 Crores, Delhi Andrews Ganj Land Scam/wrongdoings by HUDCO, and the ministry have escaped the eyes of the media.

Seven out of 10 people in India still must pay a bribe to access public services. Measures to tackle corruption and curb the growing menace of black money have dominated the national discourse over the past years. The Modi Government since 26 May 2014 has implemented many policies and legislation to get India free from corruption disease. But the bureaucracy is not making any decisions whether right or wrong and the officers are leaving the decisions to be made by the highest court, which takes half of the century to decide.

Many hidden scams are there but the present Government, despite its litigation policy, is relying on the Top Court to decide, but justice delayed is justice denied.

The Delhi Andrews Ganj Land Scam has gone without notice of CAG. In this case, the government followed another route that was "opaque and subjective". As a result, both public sector enterprise and government parted with the most controversial and precious chunk of 73 acres of land in south Delhi @ re. 1= per acre and holding monies by concealing various facts, misrepresentations, and fraud. Throughout Congress ruling for years, the Ministry of Urban Development flouted various rules and regulations.

The concerned ministry, politicians, and bureaucrats bent several rules concerning land ownership, zoning, land use, and floor-space, etc. It is on the face of how one Additional Secretary and a Secretary along with Congress Ministers and select officials placed in key posts could subvert rules and regulations to give away prime government land: a public property@Re 1= per acre.

All ministers of the Ministry of Urban Development, Ministry of Works and Housing, and Ministry of Poverty Alleviation or Ministry of Housing and Poverty Alleviation have dealt with this most prime land since the year 1950. The ministers and top bureaucrats were involved in handling this land; including inflated contracts, cheating, and other acts by them which will be exposed in the next few books on the Andrews Ganj Land Scam.

If it were a private builder who had no title of land in its favor, the construction of illegal buildings without any sanction of building plans would have resulted in the complaint he would have been going to jail. But in this case, the Government and its officers were involved.

The prime Government land was handed over to HUDCO without any approvals, or any sanctions or allotment to which was leading to another scam.

The Press clipping of Nav Bharat Times was regarding unauthorized construction by HUDCO in the Pinjrapole area. It was falsely justified that the land use comments are wrong, as per our note recorded. The remaining processes have been done by the Development Control & Planning Wing, including the critical appraisal of the report forwarded by HUDCO. Therefore, suitable comments may be formulated by the Development Control Wing concerning the decision communicated and the layout plan considered by DUAC, MCD, where Deputy Director (Zonal Planning) II was present.

But Media was controlled by the ministry not to expose the unauthorized constructions being carried out by HUDCO and instead gave false information that DUAC has approved. Municipal Corporation of Delhi had approved, although DUAC had not approved, and in any case, the layout plans submitted were conceptual. Besides, building plans were not sanctioned before the start of construction. But so, what? This is HUDCO's construction and Government work. Why should it be bothered; even if there were violations? *In my research, most of the officers did not care or were involved in the scam deliberately and intentionally*

Delhi Andrews Ganj Land Scam Book was inspired to expose the Congress government's wrongdoings. The buzz around Harshad Mehta and his mammoth exercise in investment fraud are at a fever pitch right now, thanks to Scam 1992.

People want as much information as they can get about this rags-to-riches story that saw startling highs and destructive lows. But there have been quite a few people who have been cheated by HUDCO and the financial foundation of India over the years.

As a fellow attorney, I felt it was necessary to expose the HUDCO Andrews Ganj Land scam. At the present value of Rs. 5000 crores the current circle rate, which HUDCO itself valued at Rs. 3200 Crores in the year 2012. HUDCO has profited from this scam at no cost. On 1 November 1990, the value estimate was given and totaled at Rs.42.60.

*Dear readers, Rs.42.60 paisa (Rupees forty-two and sixty paisa only) is not a typographical error. It is true and still to this year when the book is written in 2021, HUDCO Andrews Ganj Land Scam continues and remains unchecked by none of the authorities nor Courts nor the Modi Government.*

ALBORZ AZAR

In the Hudco Land Scam Series, by Alborz Azar reveals the widespread corruption behind the precious Andrews Ganj land in the heart of New Delhi. A media condemned man whose innocence remained unknown struggles with the unfounded accusations which caused public opinion to falter, leading to a guilty sentence before any trial could be scheduled.

The victim behind the scam in this situation was MS Shoes; founder Pavan Sachdeva. Behind the lies and deception, a brilliant entrepreneur took the fall for the underhanded dealings of the Hudco Land Scam.

The same man accused of underhanded dealings fulfilled his debts due to these deceptive lies, with no compensation for the legally awarded settlement. Alborz proves how Pavan's commitment not only caused financial stress on his family, but mental anxiety dealing with this issue for over two decades.

Yet, rulings go unanswered, Hudco ignores legal court findings to repay the ill-gotten monies from MS Shoes. The only response is more excuses as to why the court decisions have not been met by Hudco.

As the culprits hide in the shadows, Pavan struggled through court case after court case, proving his innocence. Official Supreme Court rulings were seen as frivolous orders to corrupt officers and business executives. Alborz brings light on the scam to reveal the truth that has deprived innocent victims of due justice for decades.

alborzaza.net

info@alborzazar.net

**HUDCO SCAM SERIES**

- **Book One:** Delhi Andrews Ganj Land Scam
- **Book Two:** Government HUDCO Andrews **Ganj Scam**
- **Book Three**: HUDCO Place **Andrews Ganj Land Scam**

- Book Four: Andrews Ganj Land Scam Continues
- **Book Five:** Bureaucrats Disputed Bjp Government Ratification of Andrews Ganj Land Scam
- **Book Six:** HUDCO Scammed Leela Hotels as Well - Refunded Entire Amount with Contractual Compounded Interest
- **Book Seven:** HUDCO Place Scam Led Andrews Ganj Project Account to Negative
- **Book Eight:** Courts Concluded HUDCO Scam Defrauded Discriminated Cheated MS Shoes
- **Book Nine:** Government Had No Time to Consider Bureaucrats Ratification of Andrews Ganj Land Scam
- **Book Ten:** Most Awaited Ratification by The Supreme Court of India Of Andrews Ganj Land Scam by HUDCO

## FALL OF MS SHOES SEIES – Pavan Sachdeva Struggling

- **BOOK ONE:** PAVAN SACHDEVA SCAM 1995: K MADHAVAN CBI FORMER JOINT DIRECTOR GAPL SOLICITOR ROLE
- **BOOK TWO:** PAVAN SACHDEVA SCAM 1995: UNDERWRITING PUBLIC ISSUE A FARCE
- **BOOK THREE:** PAVAN SACHDEVA SCAM 1995: A FALSE CASE BY CBI
- **BOOK FOUR:** PAVAN SACHDEVA SCAM 1995: MS SHOES HUDCO GOVERNMENT ANDREWS GANJ LAND
- **BOOK FOUR:** PAVAN SACHDEVA SCAM 1995: 1995 PUBLIC ISSUE AWARDS
- **BOOK FOUR:** PAVAN SACHDEVA SCAM 1995: PAVAN SACHDEVA STRUGGLING

Made in United States
Orlando, FL
04 November 2026

90215309R00144